Doing Good

Inspiring activities and ideas for young people to make the world a better place

Thomas A. Nazario and Kelly Quayle

ROWMAN & LITTLEFIELD
Lanham • Boulder • New York • London

Doing Good has been created by The Forgotten International for use by facilitators in classrooms and other settings throughout the United States in a manner in which it might most further their work with young people and adults.

Also, we do not own any rights to the videos referred to in the lessons. They are all publicly available for free online, unless otherwise noted.

Cover and interior illustrations by John Torreano (www.seraphilm.com)

Published by Rowman & Littlefield
A wholly owned subsidiary of The Rowman & Littlefield Publishing Group, Inc.
4501 Forbes Boulevard, Suite 200, Lanham, Maryland 20706
www.rowman.com

Unit A, Whitacre Mews, 26-34 Stannary Street, London SE11 4AB

Copyright © 2016 by Thomas Nazario, The Forgotten International, a 501(c)3 nonprofit organization, San Francisco, California
First Rowman & Littlefield edition published in 2017

ISBN: 978-1-4758-3246-4 (pbk. : alk. paper)
ISBN: 978-1-4758-3247-1 (electronic)

♾™ The paper used in this publication meets the minimum requirements of American National Standard for Information Sciences—Permanence of Paper for Printed Library Materials, ANSI/NISO Z39.48-1992.

Printed in the United States of America

The development of these materials was made possible by a grant from the Betsy Gordon Foundation as well as two generous gifts from Kathleen Peterson and Rocío and Michael Haas.

Dedication

Doing Good is dedicated to all those around the world who often take time out of their day to serve others. Whether it is simply to serve someone a cup of tea, to help an elderly person out of bed, to walk a child across the street, to help build a home for a homeless family, to help educate a child abroad, or to decide to give much of their wealth away to others simply because they recognize that they have far more than they need while so many around the world have so little. The motivations behind why people care and why people give of themselves may be different, but, regardless of the reasons, those who serve often truly wish to make the world a better place for all who live here. We thank them all for doing what they do.

About the Cover Image

In our modern world far too many of us spend so much time on our phones, playing video games, or simply trying to keep up with social media. The hope of this book is to move young people away from their devices and start them thinking about how to be helpful to others.

The illustration by John Torreano on the cover exemplifies just some of the ways anyone, anywhere, can "do good" in the world. It also appears on the first page of Lesson Ten, which is designed to guide young people in creating projects that will assist those in need. Whether it's through a formal local or international program or in a spontaneous moment on the street in one's own neighborhood, "doing good" can be part of one's everyday life. The activities and resources listed throughout this text are just a starting point for ideas and exploration, and the opportunities to get involved are limited only by one's imagination.

We believe that once young people begin doing good for others, as suggested by this cover image, they will make these types of experiences part of their future endeavors, and it will add joy and meaning to their lives. Moreover, caring does not require advanced degrees or a certain dollar amount; it is a gift anyone can give, anytime they wish, from wherever they are. In this way, the world we all share will be a better place.

About *Doing Good*

These materials are intended to provide coaches, educators, facilitators, and school administrators with some tools to help teach young people about problems facing the world, about caring for others, and about getting involved and making the world a better place. These materials are organized into 10 lesson plans that can be used in a classroom setting or with a specific club at school, or as part of an after-school or summer program. They can also be used by a variety of groups who simply wish to become more aware of the world around them and consider working to make the world a better place.

These materials come with additional resources, including various websites and links to be explored during the process of working with one's participants. At the conclusion of this course, it is our hope that participants would take it upon themselves to create a project that would, in one way or another, benefit those less fortunate than themselves somewhere in the world. The curriculum is intended to show participants how they can take their compassion for others to a higher level by simply taking the time to do good for others.

 Note: Most of these suggested lesson plans contain more exercises, ideas, and activities than can be completed in an hour-long session. Hence, read the lesson plans first, select those activities you wish to do in the order that makes sense to you, and proceed accordingly. Also, those exercises that you like but don't complete may be done as part of an after-school project or for homework.

Contents and Curriculum Overview

Lesson One: Gratitude

This course starts with a kind of assessment whereby participants will take a "Gratitude Quiz." The purpose of this quiz is to see how many of the participants are actually thankful for the lives they lead, and if so, what level of gratitude they express. Since some of the participants in this program may lead relatively privileged lives, it is our hope that, at least to some degree, participants will recognize the advantages they have and will be thankful for them. Some time will also be dedicated to conveying to the participants the purpose of this lesson and course and the hope that, over the time together, participants will work to make a positive difference in the lives of some people in need.

Lesson Two: The Real World

This lesson starts with a quiz titled "How Much Do You Know about the World We Live In?" The purpose of this lesson is to give the participants a broader perspective about the world in which we live.

Lesson Three: The Problems We Face

This lesson seeks to inform participants of the world's greatest problems and the challenges we face as delineated in the United Nations Millennium Report. These are challenges that young people will be forced to face in their lifetime, and therefore should know more about and begin to think about how best we might try to find solutions to some of them in an effort to make the world a better place.

Lesson Four: Empathy

This lesson is devoted to exploring the meaning of empathy and how empathy differs from sympathy or pity. Participants will likely also discover that in many cases, it is the empathy that one may feel for another that often drives one to want to help.

In this lesson, participants will explore the concept and practice of compassion. They will examine how compassion has been defined and demonstrated by various historical figures and recognize the power of compassion, both in how it is expressed in our daily lives and in the larger context of doing good in the world. Finally, participants will hopefully commit to the deliberate practice of compassion or kindness to others in their own lives.

Since the work of The Forgotten International is largely about poverty and the alleviation of poverty, in this lesson we encourage participants to get involved in the work we do, whether that is by alleviating poverty in and around their own communities or on a global platform. For that reason, this lesson is intended to bring awareness about the extent of poverty in the world, the different types of poverty that exist, and how poverty can affect so many aspects of one's life.

This lesson is an extension of Lesson Six, but it also highlights just how simple it can sometimes be to lift one person, one family, or one village out of poverty.

This lesson will concentrate on the extent to which Americans, in general, consume so much. It is about helping participants define our wants versus our needs, and what is really important in life. Consumption, particularly overconsumption, results in much waste, which damages our environment and is caused by those of us who fail to appreciate the value of even the little things in life. Through this process, participants will begin to recognize how little so many have, while some others have far more than they need. Ideally, this might give some of the participants a different perspective on life.

Lesson Nine: Happiness

In Lesson Nine, we will attempt to sort out with participants those things that truly make people happy and share some of the recent science that has gone into the study of happiness. For example, many people believe that wealth and the acquisition of material goods have a direct impact on one's happiness. The truth is that such a correlation is at best minimal or may not be found at all. Nevertheless, it's a view that we must address in this course while, at the same time, reminding participants of some of the most effective ways to live happy lives, one of which is by demonstrating kindness and generosity toward others.

Lesson Ten: Doing Good

This lesson is a transitional one, and here participants will begin to conceptualize or decide on a project that will actualize the doing of good and, in the process, come up with a plan to help others. This may involve working with a facilitator or mentor, working with the community, or working separately in teams. Nevertheless, participants have to tackle an issue related to poverty and work together to help those in need. In return, they will feel better about themselves and the contribution they have made. Hopefully it is a lesson that will stay with them throughout their lives.

The young people who received and participated in the above curriculum now are encouraged to create and execute a service project for members of their local and/or global community in need. With the knowledge of the kinds of problems that exist and how simple acts of kindness can, in fact, make positive changes in the world around us, young people can become active contributors in helping to find solutions to issues they see around them. Again, our hope is that they make giving and caring part of their lives as they get older and eventually pass that approach to life on to their own children.

Appendices: Ideas & Resources

Lesson One: Gratitude

" *Gratitude unlocks the fullness of life. It turns what we have into enough, and more. It turns denial into acceptance, chaos to order, confusion to clarity. It can turn a meal into a feast, a house into a home, a stranger into a friend. Gratitude makes sense of our past, brings peace for today, and creates a vision for tomorrow.* **"**

~ Melody Beattie

Who Is Melody Beattie?

Melody Beattie is one of America's most beloved authors, specializing in addiction and recovery. She has survived abandonment, kidnapping, sexual abuse, drug and alcohol addiction, divorce, and the death of a child. Ms. Beattie has made her life's mission to teach others the lessons she has learned. Through her writings and talks, she helps others who are enduring similar challenges in life while encouraging them to express gratitude for what they have been given instead of focusing on what has been lost.

LESSON ONE: PRINCIPAL OBJECTIVE

Since this is the first lesson of the program, it is important to introduce yourself and have the participants introduce themselves. Give the participants some sense of what this program is all about, what the lessons might entail, and what the ultimate goal might be. Please do not give away too much, for some surprises are always nice, and to some extent participants might feel offended if told that this course, and in particular this first class, has been designed to help them appreciate what they have and be more generous to others. Some participants may already feel quite appreciative and may feel that it is presumptuous of us to think otherwise. Also, we should see ourselves as facilitators rather than instructors, and remember that the good that comes out of this course work will be good that comes from the participants' hearts and minds and should not be a product of teachers leading them by the nose or forcing them to do something that they would rather not do.

ADDITIONAL OBJECTIVES

✔ Participants will evaluate and reflect on the extent to which they are grateful for their gifts in life.

✔ Participants will recognize the discrepancy between what resources they have and the resources available to millions of others.

✔ Participants will discuss the people and things they are grateful for in life.

✔ Participants will express gratitude to people in their lives who support them.

As you proceed through this lesson, it is extremely important that you keep in mind that we should never believe that simply because a young person has many material possessions or has been given the opportunity to attend a fine school or lives in a nice house that he or she has experienced much joy in his or her life. Also, we should not assume that participants are particularly grateful for all they have, even though on the surface one would think that they should be very grateful for "all" that they have been given. The way one feels at any particular time may not be all that rational. Nevertheless, these feelings are genuine and need to be respected.

Quite "privileged" youth are often not that happy. They may, in fact, lack support, lack affection, or even have been abused or neglected. So walk carefully through these exercises and if you get the impression that all is not well through what is revealed to you, investigate it further, for sometimes a lack of gratitude grows out of feelings of inadequacy or out of feelings of simply being forgotten in a very meaningful way by those who should be supporting us. It is important to try to figure out how and why participants have come to their conclusions and feelings before thinking that they are simply naive or ungrateful.

Activity #1: Quiz "Some Questions to Consider about Your Life and the World Around You" (10 minutes)

Distribute handout and have your participants take this quiz. **(Handout 1-A)**

Facilitators should see how to evaluate this exercise. **(Handout 1-B)**

 Note: This quiz/exercise is largely for the facilitator's own use and should be helpful to him or her in assessing the degree to which participants are grateful for the lives they lead and/or realize to what extent they have been blessed. It is a simple starting point and no more, although it could be argued that it might be those participants who are least aware of their blessings have the most to learn and possibly gain through this course and program. They may also be the hardest participants to reach.

Activity #2: Checking Pulse (15 minutes)

In partners, have participants ask each other the following questions and discuss among themselves. Allot a limited amount of time to each partner.

Initial Questions:

* *How is your day going so far?*

* *How are you feeling today?* (Participants can't simply answer "good" but must respond in words that express emotion—for example, happy, tired, stressed, excited, frustrated or mad.)

* Discuss for a short time. Partners switch.

Next questions:

* *When was the last time you felt really frustrated or disappointed by something or someone? What happened?*

* *Is there anything you feel you are denied by either your teachers or the people who take care of you?*

* Discuss for a short time. Partners switch.

Final questions:

* *What is something that happened today that you are grateful for?*

* *What is something someone did for you recently that was nice?*

* *When was the last time you felt really grateful for something? What was that?*

* Discuss for a short time. Partners switch.

DEBRIEF:

Here, the facilitator should ask participants (as either a full class share-out or free-write) follow-up questions, such as:

- *How many people said their day was going well? Going badly?*

- *How many people used positive adjectives to describe how they were feeling? Negative adjectives?*

- *How easy was it to think of something that frustrated you? How long did it take you?*

- *How easy was it to think of something that you were grateful for? How long did it take you?*

Note: The most effective lessons are ones in which people arrive at insights on their own. This activity works well to facilitate "ah-ha" moments that lead to further contemplation such as *"Why was it so much easier for me to start complaining than to think of something I'm grateful for?"* It plants a seed for the rest of program.

Activity #3: How Lucky Are You? (20–25 minutes)

Write the following question on the board: *Do you consider yourself lucky?*

Distribute **Handout 1-C** to participants and give them at least five minutes to answer the Yes/No questions.

Sample Questions:

- *Did you eat dinner last night?*

- *Have you ever woken up and wished you didn't have to go to school?*

- *If you get sick, can you see a doctor?*

For information about these sample questions, see **Handout 1-D**, which reveals how their answers match up with the rest of the world.

Here, also consider viewing the video **"First World Problems Anthem"** by WaterisLife.com (1 minute)
www.youtube.com/watch?v=fxyhfiCO_XQ

Note: The point of this activity is to get participants to recognize many of the basic necessities in life they take for granted. The use of the video is important because research shows that people respond more empathically when they are dealing with real people instead of just numbers or statistics. Another purpose of this activity is to hopefully create in participants a sense of inter-connectivity between all people. Statistics alone cannot achieve this.

DEBRIEF:

After participants have done the above exercise and have watched the video, do a free-write debrief or a class share-out as to their thoughts and or realizations.

Activity #4: Who Supports Me? (5–10 minutes)

Have participants write out a list of people who support them. For each person, ask them to answer: *When was the last time you said thank you to them?* Discuss responses and consider alternatives or follow-up questions. For example:

- *Who is someone in your life for whom you feel gratitude?*
- *How do they support you?*
- *Why are you grateful for them?*
- *Do you express your gratitude to them?*
- *Is it important to express gratitude? Why?*
- *How do you thank them?*

Activity #5: Expressing Gratitude (optional)

This can be as big or little as you like and can also be given as homework. Here, participants are to write thank-you letters to people who support them. This can be done in different ways. Some examples:

• Pocket Thank-You

Give participants small squares of paper on which they will write a "pocket thank-you" in one to three lines expressing thanks to someone. The idea is that they will later slip the thank-you in the person's pocket/locker/bag/car. Participants can do as many of these as they like, or as time allows. They should, however, try to write down why that person is being thanked. For example, *"Thank you for always giving me a hug when you can tell I'm having a bad day."*

• A Thank-You Letter

Give participants a meaningful amount of time to write out a heartfelt letter to someone in their life who supports them tremendously but whom they've never thanked or never thanked enough. In the letter, the participant should try to lay out everything the person does to support him or her. Typically this would be written to a family member, a teacher, a coach, or a best friend.

Activity #6: Video "No Arms, No Legs, No Worries" by Nick Vujicic (optional)

Watch this video with participants and discuss what is the message of this video. What do they think of this young man's attitude toward life? There are multiple videos by and about Nick Vujicic. Here is a 4-minute edit by HumplePie Ent.
www.youtube.com/watch?v=ciYk-UwqFKA

Activity #7: Revisit the Gratitude Quiz (optional)

Have participants revisit their Gratitude Quiz **(Handout 1-A)**. At this point, the participants have spent 50 minutes examining gratitude in their lives and should have a somewhat different understanding of what gratitude means and all that they may take for granted. Give them the opportunity to change their answers to more accurately reflect how they practice gratitude in their daily lives.

Activity #8: Video "Gratitude" (optional)

A very nice way to end this lesson is to have your group watch the video **"Gratitude"** by Gratitude HDMoving Art™ (6 minutes). It's a beautiful piece that illustrates how important it is to simply stop and appreciate the little things and the gift that every day holds.
www.youtube.com/watch?v=nj2ofrX7jAk

Activity #9: A Gratitude Journal (optional)

Every night for the following week, ask participants to make a list of at least two things or people for which they are grateful. As participants work on their list, have them always keep in mind: How are they expressing their thanks to people (if at all)? Have them think about whether they wish to do more to thank those who have helped them throughout their life. If so, have them act on it.

A simpler way to accomplish many of these same goals is to ask participants to make a list of the things they appreciate most in life and to simply make an effort in the future to count their blessings. Participants may choose to keep a Gratitude Journal or Compassion Journal for the entire program to have a place to note their thoughts, feelings, and emotions for each lesson.

Handouts Lesson One: *Gratitude*

Handout 1-A
The Gratitude Quiz: Some Questions to Consider about Your Life and the World Around You

Handout 1-B
Evaluating the Gratitude Quiz

Handout 1-C
Quiz: Have You Ever Thought about These Aspects of Your Life?

Handout 1-D
Reflections on "Have You Ever Thought about These Aspects of Your Life?"

Handout 1-A

The Gratitude Quiz: Some Questions to Consider
about Your Life and the World Around You (from HappierHuman.com)

Using the scale below as a guide, write the number beside each of these statements that best indicates how much you agree with the statement.

1 = strongly disagree

2 = disagree

3 = slightly disagree

4 = neutral

5 = slightly agree

6 = agree

7 = strongly agree

1. I have so much in life to be thankful for. _____

2. If I made a list of everything that I felt grateful for, it would be a very long list. _____

3. When I look at the world today, I don't see much to be grateful for. _____

4. I am grateful to a wide variety of people. _____

5. As I get older, I find myself more able to appreciate the people, events, and situations that have been part of my life history. _____

6. Long amounts of time can go by before I feel grateful for something or to someone. _____

Handout 1-B

Evaluating the Gratitude Quiz

Here is an example of a score one might produce if one is quite grateful for his or her life:

Question 1. I have so much in life to be thankful for. (7)

Question 2. If I made a list of everything that I felt grateful for, it would be a very long list. (7)

Question 3. When I look at the world today, I don't see much to be grateful for. (1)

Question 4. I am grateful to a wide variety of people. (7)

Question 5. As I get older, I find myself more able to appreciate the people, events and situations that have been part of my life history. (7)

Question 6. Long amounts of time can go by before I feel grateful for something or to someone. (1)

When grading this quiz, you need to add the numbers associated with Questions #1, #2, #4, and #5, and then add the total of the numbers associated with Questions #3 and #6. Now subtract the total for Questions #3 and #6 from the total for Questions #1, #2, #4, and #5. The highest score (people who express the greatest amount of gratitude) one can achieve on this quiz is **26**. The lowest score would be a **-10**.

If participants put a (3), (4), or (5) for the majority of their answers, then they will most likely have a fairly low gratitude rating since they are only slightly agreeing or disagreeing and therefore do not feel very strongly about anything they have in their life, whether good or bad. This means they most likely feel they live a very ordinary or below-average life.

Handout 1-C

Quiz: Have You Ever Thought about These Aspects of Your Life?

Circle your answer

1. When you go home, do you have a warm and comfortable house to live in?
   Yes or No

2. Throughout your life, has there always been someone around to look after you?
   Yes or No

3. Do you have a refrigerator at your home?
   Yes or No

4. Do you have food in your refrigerator?
   Yes or No

5. Are you sometimes given a little money to buy yourself a snack, special item, or gift?
   Yes or No

6. If you get sick or hurt, do you have a doctor or a hospital that you can go to?
   Yes or No

7. Do you have a shower at home, and does it provide you with clean hot water?
   Yes or No

8. When you were small, did you have to get all your shots and drops (immunizations) before you started school?
   Yes or No

9. If you wake up in the middle of the night and have to go to the bathroom, do you have to leave your home?
   Yes or No

10. Do you ever regret having to go to school?
    Yes or No

11. Are you planning to go to college someday?
    Yes or No

12. Have you ever taken a vacation with some friends or family or have traveled on an airplane?
    Yes or No

Handout 1-D

Reflections on "Have You Ever Thought about These Aspects of Your Life?"

1. When you go home, do you have a warm and comfortable house to live in?

At least 1.6 billion people around the world live in inadequate housing. This often means a home with no or little heat, no electricity, no running water, and no real protection from various vermin, insects, or diseases. Of these children and families, 100 million individuals are completely homeless. **"Press Briefing by Special Rapporteur on Right to Adequate Housing" (www.un.org/News/briefings/docs/2005/kotharibrf050511.doc.htm)**

2. Throughout your life, has there always been someone around to look after you?

Throughout the world there are as many as 59 million children and many more adults who, for much of their lives, have grown up on the streets without anyone to care for them. Children who have no one to care for them and may live on the street, of course, face many risks daily that in some cases take their lives. Also, children who have places to come home to do not necessarily have people around to look after them. Child neglect is the most common type of child abuse in the world, and although neglect can take many forms, one of the most prevalent forms of child neglect is physical neglect, which includes abandonment or the desertion of a child without arranging for their reasonable care. **"Child Welfare Information Gateway: Child Abuse and Neglect" (www.childwelfare.gov/topics/systemwide/statistics/can/)**

3. Do you have a refrigerator at your home?

Although the exact number of people who live without refrigeration is unknown, a quarter of humanity—1.6 billion people—lives without electricity. Of this staggering number, most live in South Asia and Sub-Saharan Africa. **(www.globalissues.org/article/26/poverty-facts-and-stats)** Without access to energy, people often cannot improve their standard of living. Also, these same impoverished people often get no relief from the sweltering heat in their regions. **(www.worldbank.org/en/topic/energy)**

4. Do you have food in your refrigerator?

Global hunger or malnutrition is not a recent phenomenon; yet it is an issue that continues to plague many people today. Malnutrition results from the insufficient intake of nutrients into the body. What may start out as hunger can lead to chronic malnutrition and, in severe cases, acute malnutrition and death. Acute malnutrition occurs when the body does not receive the routine nourishment it needs to produce energy and begins to consume its own tissues in search of an energy source. Approximately 55 million children suffer from acute malnutrition worldwide. Of the 55 million, 19 million children experience its deadliest form. Acute malnutrition is responsible for 3.5 million child deaths each year. Hence, refrigerated food that one can access at any time is truly a blessing. **(www.actionagainsthunger.org/hunger)**

Continued on next page

Reflections on "Have You Ever Thought about These Aspects of Your Life?"

5. Are you sometimes given a little money to buy yourself a snack, special item, or gift?

Your parents might give you anywhere from $1 to $5 to buy a snack or lunch each day at school. They might give you $20 for the shirt that you've been wanting. But did you know that half the world, approximately 3 billion people, lives on less than $2.50 per day? This leaves these people and their children with little or no extra income for any kind of "extras" you may have personally grown accustomed to. **(www.globalissues.org/article/26/poverty-facts-and-stats)**

6. If you get sick or hurt, do you have a doctor or hospital that you can go to?

In America, many of us take health care for granted and often argue among ourselves over how health care should be provided. However, approximately 1 billion people around the world do not have any meaningful access to health care at all. In fact, each year millions around the world who die could have been saved if they could have received even minimal care. Many of those who die are children.

7. Do you have a shower at home, and does it provide you with clean hot water?

Taking a five-minute shower uses more water than what an average person living in a developing country uses in an entire day. Approximately 780 million people (mainly in developing countries) do not have access to clean water, much less clean hot water. Furthermore, 3.4 million people die each year from a water-related disease. That's almost the entire population of the city of Los Angeles. In short, bathrooms with clean hot water and showers are luxuries that many people throughout at least half of the world have little or no access to. **"Millions Lack Safe Water" (http://water.org/water-crisis/water-sanitation-facts/)**

8. When you were small, did you have to get all your shots and drops (immunizations) before you started school?

Vaccines are a major element of modern health care and their benefits are undeniable. For example, during the late 1700s, smallpox ravaged humanity. By 1977 it was eradicated from the world due to the widespread and targeted use of vaccines. Today, more and more vaccines continue to be developed, and slowly more diseases, like polio, are reaching the brink of eradication. However, one out of every five children is still unprotected from vaccine-preventable illnesses due to insufficient funding and limited access. Furthermore, 29% of all deaths of children under age five each year, some two million children in all, occur from illnesses that could have been prevented if more vaccines could have been made available. **Immunization, "The Big Picture" (www.unicef.org/immunization/index_bigpicture.html)**

Continued on next page

Handout 1-D—*Continued from previous page:*
Reflections on "Have You Ever Thought about These Aspects of Your Life?"

9. If you wake up in the middle of the night and have to go to the bathroom, do you have to leave your home?

Believe it or not, about 40% of the world's population—2.5 billion people on earth—do not have a toilet and so must go outside to relieve themselves. In short, they lack any kind of a modern bathroom facility.

10. Do you ever regret having to go to school?

For many around the world, getting the opportunity to go to school is a privilege. This is particularly true for young girls. At present, about 70 million school age children around the world wake up every day without the opportunity to go to school. Also, 57% of primary school-age children in the developing world who are not in school are girls. **"Global Campaign for Education" (http://image.guardian.co.uk/sys-files/Education/documents/2010/09/20/1Goal.pdf)**

11. Are you planning to go to college someday?

Only 4–8% of the world's youth ever make it to college or advance beyond secondary education. Hence, those who get to go are quite lucky.

12. Have you ever taken a vacation with some friends or your family or traveled on an airplane?

Taking a vacation, getting on an airplane, and escaping everyday life is a luxury that only very fortunate people enjoy. In fact, any kind of vacation is way out of reach for more than half of the world's people. That is because approximately 80% of the world's population makes only $10 a day or less, and that money goes toward purchasing the necessities of life, not vacations. Moreover, only 4–5% of the world's people have ever traveled by airplane.

Lesson Two: The Real World

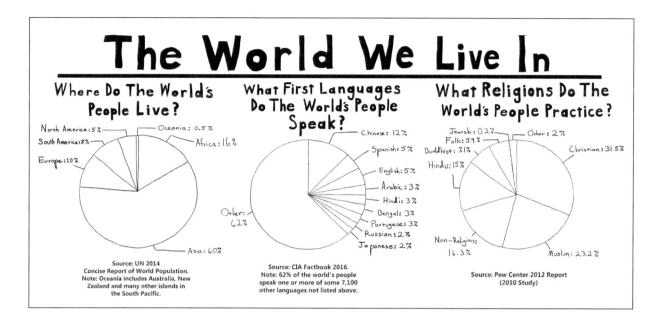

The World We Live In

Where Do The World's People Live?

- North America: 5%
- South America: 8%
- Europe: 10%
- Oceania: 0.5%
- Africa: 16%
- Asia: 60%

Source: UN 2014 Concise Report of World Population. Note: Oceania includes Australia, New Zealand and many other islands in the South Pacific.

What First Languages Do The World's People Speak?

- Chinese: 12%
- Spanish: 5%
- English: 5%
- Arabic: 3%
- Hindi: 3%
- Bengali: 3%
- Portugese: 3%
- Russian: 2%
- Japanese: 2%
- Other: 62%

Source: CIA Factbook 2016. Note: 62% of the world's people speak one or more of some 7,100 other languages not listed above.

What Religions Do The World's People Practice?

- Jewish: 0.2%
- Folk: 5.9%
- Buddhist: 7.1%
- Hindu: 15%
- Other: 2%
- Christian: 31.5%
- Muslim: 23.2%
- Non-Religious: 16.3%

Source: Pew Center 2012 Report (2010 Study)

The Paradox of Our Age

" We have bigger houses, but smaller families; more conveniences, but less time;
we have more degrees, but less sense; more knowledge, but less judgment;
more experts, but more problems; more medicines, but less healthiness.
We've been all the way to the moon and back,
but have trouble crossing the street to meet the new neighbor.
We've built more computers to hold more information,
to produce more copies than ever, but we have less communication;
we have become long on quantity, but short on quality.
These are times of fast foods, but slow digestion;
tall man, but short character; steep profits, but shallow relationships.
It's a time when there is much in the window, but nothing in the room. "

~ His Holiness the 14th Dalai Lama

Who Is the Dalai Lama?

His Holiness the 14th Dalai Lama is the spiritual leader of Tibet, a region in China. He has long practiced Tibetan Buddhism and conducts many teachings around the world. He is thought to be one of the world's kindest individuals and the Buddha of Compassion. The words "Dalai Lama" mean "an ocean of wisdom." So, too, much of what he teaches comes from a lifetime of study and meditation about the world we live in and how we can all build a meaningful and happy life for ourselves and others.

LESSON TWO: PRINCIPAL OBJECTIVE

This lesson is intended to bring participants to the next level of study. In Lesson One they learned about gratitude and were hopefully impressed by some of the blessings that they have in life, but possibly failed to realize. The purpose of this lesson is to give the participants some perspective about the world in general as well as to possibly help free them from a narrow sense of the world they may have, either because they have lived in a rather sheltered environment or because thay have been largely preoccupied with television shows or video games that have failed to expose them to the real world.

ADDITIONAL OBJECTIVES

✔ Participants will test their knowledge of global issues.

✔ Participants will participate in a wealth distribution simulation.

✔ Participants will learn important facts about the world and its diverse human population.

✔ Participants will reflect on similarities shared across cultures and continents and hopefully recognize that we are all members of the human family.

Part I

Activity #1: Quiz "How Much Do You Know about the World We Live In?" (15 minutes)

Participants here are asked to take a quiz that tests their knowledge of some basic world facts.

Give them 10–15 minutes. **(Handout 2-A)**

After participants complete the quiz, have them trade tests with a classmate and then go over the test with the full class, using the Answer Key, to elaborate on the various questions and answers. **(Handout 2-B)**

Ask participants which answers surprised them, and further unpack commonly missed questions. Participants should not feel bad if they missed many of the answers. This is about learning about global issues that may be new to most participants. For this reason, you may choose to have participants review their own answers. Please do, however, review the Answer Key with them, and if you wish, you can make a copy of the answers for the participants.

Activity #2: Wealth and/or Food Distribution Simulation

(15 minutes)

 Note: This activity requires the use of something tangible to simulate money or food. A good suggestion would be using Hershey's Kisses or some similar wrapped candies because they are easily distributed. This activity would require at least two large bags of such candy. It also requires that you convert statistics as to wealth or food in given countries when distributing these treats. Round up or down when necessary.

After gathering up the candy and the participants, break the group into three small groups. One group should represent the people who live in countries of the developed world (for example, United States, United Kingdom, or Germany). The second group should represent the people of a developing country (for example, Brazil, South Korea, or Mexico). The third group should represent the people of a least developed country (for example, Cambodia, Ethiopia, or Liberia).

Here is where you would have to do some research and decide whether you would like to distribute candy to these groups in amounts equivalent to the income that average individuals earn in these countries annually or an amount of food or calories that they consume or have access to daily.

For example, the average young person growing up in the United States may have access to, and in fact consume, a considerable amount of food annually (three or four meals a day); hence they would be given the equivalent of 20 pieces of candy, as opposed to the average child in Ethiopia, who is fed almost nothing on a given day, and hence he or she may only get two pieces of candy. Participants who live in countries in the middle may get somewhere between eight and twelve pieces of candy. This would show participants how food or wealth and opportunities in life are not shared equally among the world's people, and what you are lucky enough to be given over the course of your life depends, in part, on where you are born, to whom you may be born, or where you live. Hence, life in large part is an accident of birth and has little to do with what might be just. If participants feel cheated or angry about what some participants were given as opposed to what others received, that is what this exercise is about. Life is not always fair.

DEBRIEF:

Afterward, ask the participants questions such as:

What were your reactions to this activity? What surprised you the most? Why do you think we did this activity? How do you feel about the amount of food/money your group received?

 Note: When participants answer a question, make sure they identify what country they represented during the activity.

Ways to Further Critical Thinking (optional)

What about the psychological consequences of wealth inequality? Did the participants with a lot of candy enjoy the activity more? Did they feel superior in some way to those who were given less? Did they offer to share their riches with others, and if so, did they share equally or only with their friends?

Apply these observations to the real world. How do the participants' behaviors resemble (or not resemble) the real world?

Three Variations on Activity #2

1. Another possibility to consider here is to break up a group based on population. To do so, take a group of 20 participants to the front of the room and divide them among the six major continents in the world according to how the world's population is distributed on Earth. If this were done, the group would look like this:

- Asia would have a population of 12 participants
- Africa would have a population of 3 participants
- Europe would have a population of 2 participants
- North America would have a population of 1 participant (really 1.4 participants)
- South America would have a population of 1 participant
- Australia would have a population of 1 participant (really 0.3 participants)

Hence, if one sorts out this group in this manner, participants will get a visual of where the world's people live.

 If you do this version of this activity, consider having the group watch a video titled **"The Miniature Earth. 2010 edition, official version"** and debrief it afterward. **https://youtube.com/watch?v=i4639vev1Rw** (3 minutes)

2. If you take these same continents and distribute to the participants based on which continent they live in and have candy represent the average per capita wealth of individuals in these continents, the distribution would look like this:

- Asia's 12 participants would get 13 pieces of candy to share between them
- Africa's 3 participants would share two pieces of candy
- Europe's 2 participants would share 30 pieces of candy
- North America's 1 participant would get 35 pieces of candy
- South America's 1 participant would get 14 pieces
- Australia's 1 participant would get 5 pieces

3. You could also decide to hand out 100 chocolate bars according to how wealth is distributed throughout the world regardless of where these people happen to live. Using a group of 20, 2 participants who would be in the top 10% of the world's wealthiest people would share 80 bars of chocolate. Of the 40% of the world in the middle wealth brackets, 9 participants would get 19 bars of chocolate to share, while 50% of the world's population and poorest people on earth, or 10 participants, would have to all share one chocolate bar.

Note: Activity #2, in all its variations, is quite enlightening. Be prepared for a lot of questions and try to bring home the message about just how unevenly the world's resources and wealth are distributed among the people of the world.

Part II

But We Are All the Same: Showing Common Humanity

It is important to balance out the activities above with the activities below that demonstrate our similarities, for one of the main purposes of this course is for participants to feel connected to the rest of the world, not set apart.

Activity #3: T-chart Brainstorm Difference/Similarities
(6 minutes)

Here, have participants brainstorm ways in which the people of these different continents are the same and ways in which they are different. What should come out of this activity is that we all share things such as abilities, needs, emotions, and dreams, and all that sets us apart are language, culture, and resources. So, in the end, are all people more similar than different?

Activity #4: Reflection (4 minutes)

At the close of class, participants might discuss and reflect on the day's lesson. What insights did they come away with? How do you explain the inequality?

Activity #5: Video "Call Me Hope" by Mamahope.org (optional)

Just for fun, watch **"Call Me Hope"** (2 minutes). This video speaks to the beauty and diversity of the human family. **www.youtube.com/watch?v=OzQfFcy3KJg**

Activity #6: Video "The Sharing Experiment" by Action Against Hunger (optional)

This video shows how young children solve the problem of inequality. At what point did we "unlearn" how to share? **https:www.youtube.com/watch?v=zFTspq_nzG4** (2 minutes)

23

Handouts Lesson Two: The Real World

Handout 2-A
Quiz: How Much Do You Know about the World We Live In?

Handout 2-B
Answer Key: How Much Do You Know about the World We Live In?

Handout 2-A

How Much Do You Know about the World We Live In?

Circle the correct answer

(Question #12, simply give us your opinion)

1. How many people live on this planet?

a) 700 million

b) 3 billion

c) 7 billion

d) 20 billion

2. How big is a billion?

a) It equals a million 10 times over

b) It equals a million 100 times over

c) It equals a million 1000 times over

d) It equals a million a million times over

3. What percentage of the people who live on this planet live in the United States?

a) 1%

b) 6%

c) 20%

d) 45%

4. Which country is the most populated country in the world?

a) The United States

b) India

c) Russia

d) China

5. What country has the largest number of impoverished people?

a) Mexico

b) China

c) The United States

d) India

6. What kills more children under the age of 5 each year than anything else?

a) The lack of clean water

b) The lack of clean food

c) The lack of medical care

d) Poverty

7. Which statement is true about boys and girls?

a) More boys are born and brought into the world each year than girls.

b) More girls are born and brought into the world each year than boys.

c) Boys and girls are born at equal rates.

d) The gender of those who are born each year varies, so it is impossible to make a general statement as to the answer to this question.

8. What is the *primary* role of the United Nations?

a) To encourage the countries of the world to cooperate in meaningful dialogues and, in doing so, try to bring about world peace.

b) To deal with natural disasters and work to save lives whenever possible.

c) To guard against economic and market collapses around the world.

d) All of the above

9. What race has the greatest number of people on earth?

a) Asians

b) Caucasians

c) Blacks

d) Mixed Race

10. What country has the greatest number of billionaires?

a) The United States

b) China

c) England

d) India

11. What country and its people are the most charitable?

a) The Netherlands

b) Australia

c) The United States

d) Greece

12. What country is the greatest country in the world?

_____

Explain why you feel this way: _____

_____

_____

Handout 2-B

Answer Key: How Much Do You Know about the World We Live In?

1. Correct Answer: C) 7 billion

The world's present population is slightly over 7 billion. We reached that mark on October 31, 2011. Our population, of course, continues to grow. This website shows the changing numbers in the world's population and how it changes minute to minute.

See: www.worldometers.info

 Note: According to the chief population analyst in the United Nations, these estimates are based on fertility, mortality, and migration information gathered by government censuses, independent demographic and health surveys, official birth and death record, and academic studies. UN analysts revise their numbers every five years and by 2050, it is estimated that there will likely be 10 billion people on Earth.

2. Correct Answer: C) A billion is a million 1,000 times over

This is a question people often get wrong because a lot of people are afraid of math and numbers, but in just the same way that a million is 1,000 times bigger than a thousand, a billion is 1,000 times bigger than a million.

3. Correct Answer: B) 6%

This answer usually surprises people because when one grows up in the United States we often get the impression that we are bigger or are more dominant than we truly are. In reality, only 1 out of about 17 people on Earth is from the United States. This website measures the changing population status of the world, including the United States.

See: www.census.gov/popclock

4. Correct Answer: D) China

Though not the largest country in area, it is the largest in population with almost 1.4 billion people.

See: www.census.gov/popclock

5. Correct Answer: D) India

India is the second most populated country in the world with about 1.1 billion people. Unfortunately about 400,000,000 of them live in extreme poverty. Hence, of the world's poor, one third of them live in India alone.

6. Correct Answer: D) Poverty

Below are some facts that relate to this question. However, the best answer to this question is poverty because of the children around the world who die before their fifth birthday, nearly all of

Continued on next page

them are extremely poor, and it is their poverty that reduces their chances of combating many of the specific factors that kill them.

Key facts:

- Worldwide, about 7 million children under the age of five die each year.
- More than half of these early child deaths are due to conditions that could be prevented or treated with access to simple, affordable interventions.
- Leading causes of death in children under five are pneumonia, preterm birth complications, diarrhea, birth asphyxia, and malaria. Also, at least one-third of all of these child deaths are linked to malnutrition.
- Children in Sub-Saharan Africa are about 16.5 times more likely to die before the age of five than children in the developed world.

See: WHO: "Children: Reducing Mortality"
www.who.int/mediacentre/factsheets/fs178/en

7. Correct Answer: A) More Boys than Girls

Most of us would assume there are an equal number of boys and girls born every day, but nature has another plan. Worldwide, there are 107 boy babies born for every 100 girl babies. This skewed ratio is partly due to sex-selective abortion and "gendercide," the killing of female infants, in countries such as China and India where males are more desired. But even discounting those factors, the completely natural male-to-female sex ratio still hovers around 105 to 100, meaning that women are inherently more likely to give birth to boys. Why?

There seem to be several factors that influence whether a sperm containing a Y sex chromosome or one containing an X chromosome will be first to fertilize an egg, including parental ages, their environmental exposure, stress, the stage in the mother's ovulation cycle, and even whether she has had children previously. All these forces combine to set the average sex ratio at fertilization at 105 to 100. But what good is this built-in bias?

Many demographers have speculated that the gender imbalance at birth may be evolution's way of evening things out overall, for male infants more often suffer from health complications than female infants. This disadvantage runs to adulthood, as adult men kill each other more often, take more risks, and have more health problems, on average, than women, all of which cause them to die younger. This doesn't balance the sex scales exactly, but it does come close, for among the total human population, the ratio of men to women is 101 to 100.

See: "Why Are More Boys Born Than Girls?"
www.livescience.com/33491-male-female-sex-ratio.html

"Climate Change Could Alter the Human Male-Female Ratio"
www.livescience.com/48070-male-fetus-climate-change.html

Continued on next page

Handout 2-B—Continued from previous page:
Answer Key: *How Much Do You Know about the World We Live In?*

8. Correct Answer: A) World Peace

The United Nations officially came into existence on October 24, 1945, when the UN Charter was ratified by a majority of the original 51 member states. The day is now celebrated each year around the world as United Nations Day. At that time, the purpose of the United Nations was to bring all nations of the world together to work for peace and development, based on the principles of justice, human dignity, and the well-being of all people. It affords the opportunity for countries to balance global interdependence and national interests when addressing international problems. It was no accident that it was created right after World War II, for it was everyone's hope that with such a body, wars would become a thing of the past.
See: **www.un.org/en/index.html**

9. Correct Answer: A) Asians

Although many might answer that mixed race people are now the most heavily populated on earth, the correct answer still seems to be Asians. This is true because the bulk of the world's people live in East and Southeast Asia.

10. Correct Answer: A) The United States

At the last count (March 2015), *Forbes* magazine put the number of individuals worldwide who are worth a billion dollars or more at 1,826. Of that number, 526 are from the United States, so almost one-third of the world's billionaires are from this country, a country which only has 6% of the world's population. There are many reasons for this, but too many to delineate here.

Something important to note, however, is that the total wealth possessed by the world's billionaires is presently estimated to be $7.05 trillion. That is far more money than the country of India spends each year to care for over a billion people. Hence, there is a huge imbalance in the way that wealth is distributed around the world, so much so that often people question the systems that allow this to happen. Believe it or not, the top 2% of the wealthiest people in the world own over 50% of the world's total wealth while the bottom 50% own less than 1% of the world's wealth.

See: **www.forbes.com/billionaires**

11. Correct Answer: C) The United States

Since 2009, the Charities Aid Foundation has released the World Giving Index, a study of worldwide charitable behavior. In 2014, this study included more than 135 countries and more than a million interviews conducted by Gallup, and in trying to determine which are the most charitable countries in the world, they took into account these factors:

- The percentage of people who donated money to charity
- The percentage of people who volunteered their time

Continued on next page

Handout 2-B—*Continued from previous page:*
Answer Key: How Much Do You Know about the World We Live In?

- The percentage of people who helped a stranger

In doing so, they determined that in 2014 the United States and Myanmar were tied as the most charitable countries in the world.

 Note: Just so you know, The Netherlands ranks 12th on the list of most charitable countries, with Australia ranked 6th. Greece, however, ranks at 120, almost last in the world in charitable efforts.

See: **www.cafonline.org/about-us/publications/2014-publications/infographic**

12. Correct Answer: None

The answer to this question, of course, is a matter of opinion and is affected by how one would define the word "greatest." For example, would it be the country that has the best education or health care systems, the country that treats its children the best, the country with the highest standard of living, the country with the biggest military, the country with the greatest number of liberties for its citizens, or the country that seems to be the happiest or the most peaceful? Again, it depends on which measurement you use. Hence, the answer to the question is open to debate, as it is affected by one's values as to what a truly great country should do for its citizens as well as meet the needs of others in the world.

Lesson Three:
The Problems We Face

The UN Millennium Challenges

1. Poverty
2. Education
3. Equality
4. Child Health

5. Maternal Health
6. Pandemics
7. Environment
8. Global Partnership

"More than ever before in human history,

we share a common destiny.

We can master it only if we face it together.

And that is why we have the United Nations. "

~ Kofi Annan

Who Is Kofi Annan?

Kofi Annan is a Ghanaian diplomat who served as the seventh Secretary-General of the United Nations from January 1997 through December 2006. In 2001, he and the United Nations were co-recipients of the Nobel Peace Prize. Today, Kofi Annan is the founder and chair of the Kofi Annan Foundation, which works to improve global governance by focusing on promoting peace and security, sustainable development, and human rights.

LESSON THREE: PRINCIPAL OBJECTIVE

In Lesson Three, participants will be introduced to what many consider to be the world's greatest problems or, as some might say, the biggest challenges we will face in the future. These, of course, are the problems today's youth will be asked to solve. Hence, they should know a little more about the world's most pressing problems and begin to think about how best we might together try to take on some of these challenges and, in the process, make the world a better place.

ADDITIONAL OBJECTIVES

✓ Participants will learn to identify the major challenges facing the world.

✓ Participants will study the UN Millennium Report to deepen their knowledge of the world's most pressing issues.

✓ Participants will work in groups to brainstorm solutions and design a poster that demonstrates their vision of a better world.

Activity #1: Brainstorm World Problems (12 minutes)

Give participants up to 5 minutes to write down a list of what they think are the biggest problems facing the world.

Class share-out: Here the facilitator solicits answers from participants and lists them on the board. Participants will likely come up with many problems. Some will be more unique to problems we might be facing here in the United States and some might be more global in nature. After the list is complete, sort the list into groupings of one kind or another, trying to do away with redundancy, and narrow down the listings to maybe five or six big issues, challenges, or problems. Review these groupings with the participants and ask them why they have come to these conclusions.

Activity #2: The UN Millennium Report (15 minutes)

Participants study a summary of this report in pairs or small groups as they try to come up with some conclusions. See the report summary **Handout 3-A**. More information can be found at **www.un.org/millenniumgoals/**.

After participants are done, re-visit the brainstorm list on the board and add or modify ideas gleaned from the report. Also, see how many of the problems identified by the participants were also identified as major world challenges in the UN Millennium Report. Of the major problems identified in this report, those this UN body of experts felt were most pressing as we entered a new millennium were:

1. **The warming of the earth (climate change)**

2. **The continuing conflicts around the world as well as the threat of nuclear war**

3. **The continued violations of human rights around the world and the need to protect those rights**

4. **World poverty and the continued and growing economic gap between the world's rich and the world's poor**

5. **The need to provide for better health care to all the world's people as well as the need to be prepared for future pandemics**

How do the participants feel about these five areas of concern? Would they add anything to this list?

Activity #3: Watch the Video Explaining Human Rights
(15 minutes)

Watch: "What Is a Human Right?" (2 minutes)
https://www.youtube.com/watch?v=JpY9s1Agbsw

At the conclusion of this video, ask participants whether they have ever heard about the Universal Declaration of Human Rights. If the group members have little awareness about this important document, they can download a copy and handouts about it by going to this website: **www.un.org/en/universal-declaration-human-rights/index.html**. You may also simply distribute a copy of the Declaration included here as **Handout 3-B**.

Activity #4: Projects or Homework Suggestions

• **"If I Ruled the World" Poster Project**

In groups, participants are given the task: If you ruled the world, how would you make it a better place? Together, participants reflect on problems of the world and brainstorm solutions and then design a poster that demonstrates all the ways they would make the world a better place. Groups then present their posters to the larger group.

As a group, pool the best ideas from each poster to create one final list or poster. If possible, find a place where the poster might be hung.

• **$100 Million Giveaway**

Have participants work in small groups. This time tell each group that they have been given $100 million by a rich individual and they have been asked to do something with it that would benefit others in the most effective way possible. They need to decide whom they wish to help, what problem they will try to tackle, what rules they would establish so that little money is wasted and they, in fact, do something to better the world's condition. After coming up with a plan, the group will need to present that plan to the donor for approval. Each group should present their plan at the next gathering.

Have participants write an essay about the problem the world is facing that they feel is the most pressing, and why.

Handouts Lesson Three: The Problems We Face

Handout 3-A
A Summary of the United Nations Millennium Report of 2000

Handout 3-B
The Universal Declaration of Human Rights

Handout 3-A: A Summary of the United Nations Millennium Report of 2000

At the end of March 2000, then United Nations Secretary-General, Kofi Annan, released a report titled "We the Peoples—The Role of the United Nations in the 21st Century." In it he offered an action plan to try to improve the lives of many of the world's people. This report has become known as the Millennium Report. The report itself set goals and targets to be reached by certain dates. It was released in the year 2000 in the hopes that the world would view the turn of the century, as well as the fact that we were entering a new millennium, as a unique opportunity and time to make a positive change in the world's condition.

The drafter of this report was particularly concerned about the fact that the world was in many ways getting smaller through the advent of globalization, technology, and simple growth in population. As such, we were experiencing new challenges related to crime, narcotics, terrorism, pollution, disease, war, and weapons of mass destruction, as well as an influx of refugees into cities and across borders. Added to this was the fact that while globalization and world trade was bettering the standard of living for many, its benefits were not being equally shared and, as a result, had caused an increasing wealth gap among the world's people.

So, in addition to stating that more efforts will, from this moment on, be placed on issues related to climate change, better global stewardship, world peace, human rights, disease, and global health concerns, particularly regarding those issues that impact greatly those most vulnerable, the United Nations stated that it wished to create a world "free from want." In doing so, it noted that although the past half-century had seen unprecedented economic gains, 1.2 billion people were still living on less than a dollar a day, and the combination of extreme poverty with extreme inequality between individuals as well as among countries amounted to an affront to our common humanity. It was with this in mind that eight developmental goals were set out in this report, all intended to primarily benefit the poor and begin the process of helping the world's most vulnerable. Those eight goals were:

1. **Eradicate Extreme Poverty and Hunger**
2. **Achieve Universal Primary Education**
3. **Promote Gender Equality and Empower Women**
4. **Reduce Child Mortality**
5. **Improve Maternal Health**
6. **Combat HIV/AIDS, Malaria and Other Diseases**
7. **Ensure Environmental Sustainability**
8. **Global Partnership for Development**

All goals were given timelines so that measurements could be taken by world experts as to the progress that was or was not being made toward those goals. The year 2015 was a year in which many of the goals were reviewed and assessed by world bodies. How much progress has been made toward the work of bettering the lives of the world's most impoverished people?

Handout 3-B: The Universal Declaration of Human Rights

Whereas recognition of the inherent dignity and of the equal and inalienable rights of all members of the human family is the foundation of freedom, justice and peace in the world,

Whereas disregard and contempt for human rights have resulted in barbarous acts which have outraged the conscience of mankind, and the advent of a world in which human beings shall enjoy freedom of speech and belief and freedom from fear and want has been proclaimed as the highest aspiration of the common people,

Whereas it is essential, if man is not to be compelled to have recourse, as a last resort, to rebellion against tyranny and oppression, that human rights should be protected by the rule of law,

Whereas it is essential to promote the development of friendly relations between nations,

Whereas the peoples of the United Nations have in the Charter reaffirmed their faith in fundamental human rights, in the dignity and worth of the human person and in the equal rights of men and women and have determined to promote social progress and better standards of life in larger freedom,

Whereas Member States have pledged themselves to achieve, in co-operation with the United Nations, the promotion of universal respect for and observance of human rights and fundamental freedoms,

Whereas a common understanding of these rights and freedoms is of the greatest importance for the full realization of this pledge,

Now, therefore the General Assembly proclaims this Universal Declaration of Human Rights as a common standard of achievement for all peoples and all nations, to the end that every individual and every organ of society, keeping this Declaration constantly in mind, shall strive by teaching and education to promote respect for these rights and freedoms and by progressive measures, national and international, to secure their universal and effective recognition and observance, both among the peoples of Member States themselves and among the peoples of territories under their jurisdiction.

Article 1:

All human beings are born free and equal in dignity and rights. They are endowed with reason and conscience and should act towards one another in a spirit of brotherhood.

Article 2:

Everyone is entitled to all the rights and freedoms set forth in this Declaration, without distinction of any kind, such as race, color, sex, language, religion, political or other opinion, national or social origin, property, birth or other status. Furthermore, no distinction shall be made on the basis of the political, jurisdictional or international status of the country or territory to which a person belongs, whether it be independent, trust, non-self-governing or under any other limitation of sovereignty.

Continued on next page

Article 3:

Everyone has the right to life, liberty and security of person.

Article 4:

No one shall be held in slavery or servitude; slavery and the slave trade shall be prohibited in all their forms.

Article 5:

No one shall be subjected to torture or to cruel, inhuman or degrading treatment or punishment.

Article 6:

Everyone has the right to recognition everywhere as a person before the law.

Article 7:

All are equal before the law and are entitled without any discrimination to equal protection of the law. All are entitled to equal protection against any discrimination in violation of this Declaration and against any incitement to such discrimination.

Article 8:

Everyone has the right to an effective remedy by the competent national tribunals for acts violating the fundamental rights granted him by the constitution or by law.

Article 9:

No one shall be subjected to arbitrary arrest, detention or exile.

Article 10:

Everyone is entitled in full equality to a fair and public hearing by an independent and impartial tribunal, in the determination of his rights and obligations and of any criminal charge against him.

Article 11:

Everyone charged with a penal offence has the right to be presumed innocent until proved guilty according to law in a public trial at which he has had all the guarantees necessary for his defense.

No one shall be held guilty of any penal offence on account of any act or omission which did not constitute a penal offence, under national or international law, at the time when it was committed. Nor shall a heavier penalty be imposed than the one that was applicable at the time the penal offence was committed.

Continued on next page

Handout 3-B—Continued from previous page:
The Universal Declaration of Human Rights

Article 12:

No one shall be subjected to arbitrary interference with his privacy, family, home or correspondence, nor to attacks upon his honor and reputation. Everyone has the right to the protection of the law against such interference or attacks.

Article 13:

Everyone has the right to freedom of movement and residence within the borders of each state.

Everyone has the right to leave any country, including his own, and to return to his country.

Article 14:

Everyone has the right to seek and to enjoy in other countries asylum from persecution.

This right may not be invoked in the case of prosecutions genuinely arising from nonpolitical crimes or from acts contrary to the purposes and principles of the United Nations.

Article 15:

Everyone has the right to a nationality. No one shall be arbitrarily deprived of his nationality nor denied the right to change his nationality.

Article 16:

Men and women of full age, without any limitation due to race, nationality or religion, have the right to marry and to found a family. They are entitled to equal rights as to marriage, during marriage and at its dissolution.

Marriage shall be entered into only with the free and full consent of the intending spouses.

The family is the natural and fundamental group unit of society and is entitled to protection by society and the State.

Article 17:

Everyone has the right to own property alone as well as in association with others.

No one shall be arbitrarily deprived of his property.

Article 18:

Everyone has the right to freedom of thought, conscience and religion; this right includes freedom to change his religion or belief, and freedom, either alone or in community with others and in public or private, to manifest his religion or belief in teaching, practice, worship and observance.

Article 19:

Everyone has the right to freedom of opinion and expression; this right includes freedom to hold opinions without interference and to seek, receive and impart information and ideas through any media and regardless of frontiers.

Continued on next page

Article 20:

Everyone has the right to freedom of peaceful assembly and association.

No one may be compelled to belong to an association.

Article 21:

Everyone has the right to take part in the government of his country, directly or through freely chosen representatives.

Everyone has the right of equal access to public service in his country.

The will of the people shall be the basis of the authority of government; this will shall be expressed in periodic and genuine elections which shall be by universal and equal suffrage and shall be held by secret vote or by equivalent free voting procedures.

Article 22:

Everyone, as a member of society, has the right to social security and is entitled to realization, through national effort and international co-operation and in accordance with the organization and resources of each State, of the economic, social and cultural rights indispensable for his dignity and the free development of his personality.

Article 23:

Everyone has the right to work, to free choice of employment, to just and favorable conditions of work and to protection against unemployment.

Everyone, without any discrimination, has the right to equal pay for equal work.

Everyone who works has the right to just and favorable remuneration ensuring for himself and his family an existence worthy of human dignity, and supplemented, if necessary, by other means of social protection.

Everyone has the right to form and to join trade unions for the protection of his interests.

Article 24:

Everyone has the right to rest and leisure, including reasonable limitation of working hours and periodic holidays with pay.

Article 25:

Everyone has the right to a standard of living adequate for the health and well-being of himself and of his family, including food, clothing, housing and medical care and necessary social services, and the right to security in the event of unemployment, sickness, disability, widowhood, old age or other lack of livelihood in circumstances beyond his control.

Continued on next page

Handout 3-B—Continued from previous page:
The Universal Declaration of Human Rights

Motherhood and childhood are entitled to special care and assistance. All children, whether born in or out of wedlock, shall enjoy the same social protection.

Article 26:

Everyone has the right to education. Education shall be free, at least in the elementary and fundamental stages. Elementary education shall be compulsory. Technical and professional education shall be made generally available and higher education shall be equally accessible to all on the basis of merit.

Education shall be directed to the full development of the human personality and to the strengthening of respect for human rights and fundamental freedoms. It shall promote understanding, tolerance and friendship among all nations, racial or religious groups, and shall further the activities of the United Nations for the maintenance of peace. Parents have a prior right to choose the kind of education that shall be given to their children.

Article 27:

Everyone has the right freely to participate in the cultural life of the community, to enjoy the arts and to share in scientific advancement and its benefits.

Everyone has the right to the protection of the moral and material interests resulting from any scientific, literary or artistic production of which he is the author.

Article 28:

Everyone is entitled to a social and international order in which the rights and freedoms set forth in this Declaration can be fully realized.

Article 29:

Everyone has duties to the community in which alone the free and full development of his personality is possible.

In the exercise of his rights and freedoms, everyone shall be subject only to such limitations as are determined by law solely for the purpose of securing due recognition and respect for the rights and freedoms of others and of meeting the just requirements of morality, public order and the general welfare in a democratic society. These rights and freedoms may in no case be exercised contrary to the purposes and principles of the United Nations.

Article 30:

Nothing in this Declaration may be interpreted as implying for any State, group or person any right to engage in any activity or to perform any act aimed at the destruction of any of the rights and freedoms set forth herein.

Lesson Four: Empathy

"*I do not ask
the wounded person how he feels;
I myself become the wounded person.* **"**

~ Walt Whitman

LESSON FOUR: PRINCIPAL OBJECTIVE

I n this lesson, we will explore the concept of empathy and ask participants to reflect on how feelings of empathy are experienced in everyday life. They will also try to express feelings that others might be experiencing by reflecting back on times when they might have had similar feelings or might be asked to role-play what someone might be feeling as he or she goes through a difficult time in their life.

ADDITIONAL OBJECTIVES

✓ Participants will experience and express empathy and will experience how sometimes feelings of empathy drive acts of compassion.

✓ Participants will be able to articulate, in their own words, the meaning of empathy.

Activity #1: Video "Homeless Boy Steals the Talent Show" (15 minutes)

Show participants the video **"Homeless Boy Steals the Talent Show"** (8 minutes)
www.youtube.com/watch?v=tZ46Ot4_ILo
Before viewing this video, tell participants only that this video is from South Korea, and they must read the subtitles.

After viewing the video, ask participants how they felt while viewing the video. At any point did any of them cry or feel as though they were about to cry? What brought about those feelings? Can anyone say they had empathy for this boy? Can anyone define the word "empathy"? Put whatever efforts they make to define empathy on the blackboard. For a suggested definition of the word "empathy," consider the following: "The ability to feel what another person is feeling or experiencing, often feelings of sadness, despair, abandonment, frustration, or even anger. To be able to stand in the shoes of another and at least for that moment be him or her."

Note: Take a moment to distinguish the word pity or sympathy from empathy. In doing so, the facilitator might use the example of walking by a homeless woman sitting on the sidewalk in the cold rain. One who pities her may feel sorry for her and the state she is in. However, one who feels empathy for her may feel her cold and how the cold water might feel going down her hair and back. They may also know what she is thinking or asking herself. For example, "Why isn't anyone helping me?" or "I don't think I am going to make it through the night" or "I am so ashamed, I am nothing. I am invisible to everyone." Hence, this is all quite different from pity or even sympathy.

Activity #2: "Homeless" Role-Play (15 minutes)

Another way of trying to demonstrate what empathy is to the participants is to have them role-play the above situation. In short, have a participant play the role of a homeless person lying on the curb or sidewalk. He or she can do so in the corner of the classroom. Have him or her pretend to have been there for several days, hungry, tired, and disheveled. After some time alone, have him or her stand and address the group and tell the group how it feels to be ignored, about his or her life, about the lack of help, and how he or she happened to end up in that state. To make this a little easier on the person doing the role-playing, you can have the group ask him or her questions (a mock interview) and have the person who is assuming the role of the homeless person simply answer the questions. This, of course, requires that a participant place him- or herself in the mind and body of a homeless person.

When people feel the pain that others might be experiencing, some say they are more likely to come to their aid. Do your participants feel that way? Has that been true in their own lives? Can they talk about a time in their lives that they were moved to help someone they didn't know? Why did they do it? When this occurs, these actions are called "acts of compassion."

 Note: If it is possible to have guest speakers visit the group, you might reach out to a local shelter or even a social worker that works with the homeless population in the community and have them present some facts on who the homeless are among us: How many children and families make up the homeless numbers? What are some circumstances that lead to homelessness? What local resources are available to them? What are some ways to help? The participants should be given some time to ask questions.

Activity #3: Poverty Simulation Game (30 minutes)

This is an activity designed to be run in three 10-minute sessions to role-play poverty situations. **www.salvationarmy.org.nz/sites/default/files/uploads/Lesson3-Poverty-Simulation-Game-and-resources.pdf**

 ## Activity #4: Video "Children Full of Life" (optional)

A very interesting and moving documentary about empathy and caring for others is called **"Children Full of Life."** It is a five-part series of documentary shorts about how fourth graders are taught important life lessons at a school in Japan. Part One gives us a clear example of empathy.

"Children Full of Life: Part One"
www.youtube.com/watch?v=armP8TfS9Is (10 minutes)

"Children Full of Life—Important Documentary"
If you would like to view all five parts of this series, see
www.youtube.com/watch?v=1tLB1IU-H0M (40 minutes)

 # Activity #5: "Sometimes You're a Caterpillar" (optional)

Just for fun, check out this animated piece about privilege and empathy called **"Sometimes You're a Caterpillar"** (3 minutes) by Chescaleigh and Kat Blaque.
https://www.youtube.com/watch?v=hRiWgx4sHGg

Lesson Five: *Compassion*

" *Like a fly on the wall in a room in the home of His Holiness the 14th Dalai Lama, I observed His Holiness welcome a wealthy Indian gentleman and his family from the city of Mumbai, India. After 45 minutes had passed and His Holiness and this family had talked and laughed about both the little and big questions of life, the patriarch of this well-dressed and seemingly wealthy family asked the Dalai Lama if he would be so kind as to bless him and his family before they went on their way. To my surprise, His Holiness put off the request. Instead, His Holiness said, 'Who am I to bless you? I am the same as you, no better, no worse. And you are the same as I, a human being with many of the same wants and needs, just two simple friends who seek happiness and some answers to the mysteries of life. So you see, it would be silly for me to bless you, in fact you could bless me. If, however, you wish to feel blessed, please consider returning to Mumbai and when you arrive, help all those around you who have so little and suffer so much. In doing so, you will feel blessed.'* "*

~ Tom Nazario

Who Is Tom Nazario?

Professor Thomas A. Nazario teaches at the University of San Francisco, School of Law, and is the founder of the The Forgotten International, an organization that seeks to help some of the world's poorest people out of poverty. He is also an author; his most recent book is ***Living on a Dollar a Day: The Lives and Faces of the World's Poor.*** He has also co-authored this book with Ms. Kelly Quayle.

LESSON FIVE: PRINCIPAL OBJECTIVE

In this lesson, we will take the concept of empathy one step further and explore what it might mean to have compassion for others. In doing so, participants will be asked to give examples of compassion or acts of compassion and possibly talk a little about people who they believe have led lives of compassion and how they may have affected the world. At this lesson's conclusion, hopefully participants will begin to commit to trying to practice compassion in their lives and, in doing so, begin to make the world a better place.

ADDITIONAL OBJECTIVES

✔ Participants will be able to describe different levels of compassion and discuss when they have felt that they have demonstrated compassion toward others or when someone has shown some compassion toward them.

✔ Participants will think of new ways of becoming more compassionate people and possibly encourage their friends to be more giving toward others.

Activity #1: What Is Compassion? (25 minutes)

Place the question "*What is compassion?*" on the board.

Have participants take a moment to try to define this word on paper.

Pair them up with a partner and have them discuss ideas with their partner.

The facilitator then solicits ideas from participants, and together they brainstorm a definition on the board while at the same time giving some examples of compassion.

Once you have at least a loose consensus as to a definition, read the opening quote by Tom Nazario and think about compassion as suggested by the Dalai Lama. What do your participants think of what the Dalai Lama is suggesting? For some thoughts on the meaning of compassion that you might share with participants, see **Handout 5-A**.

 Note: Some believe that the world's expert on compassion is the 14th Dalai Lama, for he has studied this concept for much of his life and is considered the Buddha of Compassion. What he has said as to kindness or compassion is simply this: that there seems to be at least two levels of compassion. The first is the kindness that people should ordinarily show others regardless of their status in life, their differences of opinions, or some historical events that may have somehow affected their feelings toward each other. He goes on to say that having an open heart toward others and showing them kindness is so important in bringing peace to the world as well as to yourself. The second and higher level of compassion, however, is a level whereby people not only are kind to others but also act in some affirmative way to help relieve another person's suffering.

Activity #2: Video "22 Random Acts of Kindness" (12 minutes)

For some examples of acts of kindness or compassion, have participants view this video: **"22 Random Acts of Kindness"** (3 minutes) **www.youtube.com/watch?v=wskG18saKk0** Also show the video **"2013 Kindness Challenge Winner—Hannah Brencher, More Love Letters"** (4 minutes) **https://www.youtube.com/watch?v=h6VgNzJ04z8**

Have participants think about why people write letters of appreciation and what impact they have. If they were to write a letter to the young person in one of these videos, what would they say?

Activity #3: Thank-You Letter (15 minutes)

Have participants write a letter of thanks to someone in their lives—their parents, their teachers, their friends or family—to let the recipients know how much they are appreciated for the little and big things they do each day. It can be as short or long as the participant would like, but it should be on some kind of paper, not an email or text. Participants can even take this exercise a step further and write a letter of encouragement to a total stranger just to brighten someone's day.

Activity #4: Video "LA Man Loans His House to Homeless Family for One Year" (15 minutes)

Have participants watch this video: **www.youtube.com/watch?v=dOwMGYyGK7M** (5 minutes)

After watching this video, have participants answer these questions about what they saw:

> *What actions did this individual take to exemplify kindness?*
>
> *What did he give up or sacrifice?*
>
> *For what purpose?*
>
> *How did he make a difference in others' lives, and what did someone receive?*
>
> *Was this difference a short-term difference or a long-term difference?*
>
> *What did he receive in return for his act of compassion?*

This video serves to give participants an example of a higher level of compassion. This man performed an act not required of him but was simply motivated by a desire to help relieve the suffering of a stranger, and in doing so he gave up that which provided him with some comfort in life—his own home.

For a video that young people may relate to a little more, take a look at **"Act of Sportsmanship Gives Texas High Schooler Shot at Glory"** (3 minutes) **www.youtube.com/watch?v=5rOhn1hkkok**. It is an example of one high schooler demonstrating compassion for another. The same questions above apply.

Activity #5: Random Acts of Kindness (time varies)

Ask participants to commit at least one random act of kindness that day or over the next week. They should be prepared to report on their acts of kindness. They should make sure they record their acts as they do them, and they should write down a few words as to how such acts made them feel. This can be included in their Compassion Journal, if they decide to keep one.

Handouts Lesson Five: Compassion

Handout 5-A
Some Thoughts on the Meaning of Compassion

Handout 5-A: Some Thoughts on the Meaning of Compassion

• *"Compassion and nonviolence help us to see the enemy's point of view, to hear their questions, to know their assessment of ourselves. For from their point of view we may indeed see the basic weaknesses of our own condition, and if we are mature, we may learn and grow and profit from the wisdom of the brothers and sisters who are called the opposition."*
~ Martin Luther King Jr.

• *"Frequently people think compassion and love are merely sentimental. No! They are very demanding. If you are going to be compassionate, be prepared for action."*
~ Archbishop Desmond Tutu

• *"Let me explain what we mean by compassion. Usually, our concept of compassion or love refers to the feeling of closeness we have with our friends and loved ones. Sometimes compassion also carries a sense of pity. This is wrong—any love or compassion which entails looking down on the other is not genuine compassion. To be genuine, compassion must be based on respect for the other, and on the realization that others have the right to be happy and overcome suffering just as much as you. On this basis, since you can see that others are suffering, you develop a genuine sense of concern for them. Genuine compassion is based on the recognition that others have the right to happiness just like yourself, and therefore even your enemy is a human being with the same wish for happiness as you, and the same right to happiness as you. A sense of concern developed on this basis is what we call compassion; it extends to everyone, irrespective of whether the person's attitude toward you is hostile or friendly."* ~ The 14th Dalai Lama

• *"Our human compassion binds us the one to the other—not in pity or patronizingly, but as human beings who have learnt how to turn our common suffering into hope for the future."*
~ Nelson Mandela

• *"Compassion is not a relationship between the healer and the wounded. It's a relationship between equals. Only when we know our own darkness well can we be present with the darkness of others. Compassion becomes real when we recognize our shared humanity."*
~ Pema Chodron

• *"At the end of life we will not be judged by how many diplomas we have received, how much money we have made, how many great things we have done. We will be judged by 'I was hungry, and you gave me something to eat. I was naked and you clothed me. I was homeless, and you took me in.'"* ~ Mother Teresa

Lesson Six:
Poverty Near and Far

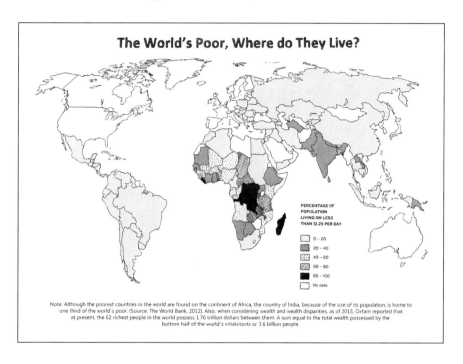

The World's Poor, Where do They Live?

PERCENTAGE OF
POPULATION
LIVING ON LESS
THAN $1.25 PER DAY

0 – 20
20 – 40
40 – 60
60 – 80
80 – 100
No data

Note: Although the poorest countries in the world are found on the continent of Africa, the country of India, because of the size of its population, is home to one third of the world's poor. (Source: The World Bank, 2012). Also, when considering wealth and wealth disparities, as of 2015, Oxfam reported that at present, the 62 richest people in the world possess 1.76 trillion dollars between them. A sum equal to the total wealth possessed by the bottom half of the world's inhabitants or 3.6 billion people.

❝ Being unwanted, unloved, uncared for, forgotten by everybody, I think that is a much greater hunger, a much greater poverty than that of the person who has nothing to eat. ❞

~ Mother Teresa

Who Was Mother Teresa?

Mother Teresa was a Catholic nun who lived in India and dedicated her life to caring for the sick and destitute. During the 1950s and 1960s she founded a powerful congregation of women who, among other things, established a leper colony, an orphanage, a nursing home, a family clinic, and a string of mobile health clinics. She received the Nobel Peace Prize in 1979 in recognition of her work in bringing help to the suffering and was recognized as a saint by the Catholic Church in 2016.

LESSON SIX: PRINCIPAL OBJECTIVE

O f the eight major world challenges identified in Lesson Three (extreme poverty, universal primary education, gender equality, child mortality, maternal healthcare, infectious diseases, environmental sustainability, and global partnerships), the one we focus on most in this lesson is poverty. The alleviation of poverty is also about doing good, demonstrating compassion, and making the world a better place. Our hope is that as participants move forward in this program, they will engage in work that helps alleviate world poverty and the suffering that poverty brings to so many. This lesson begins that process by bringing some awareness to participants about the extent of poverty and the different kinds of poverty.

ADDITIONAL OBJECTIVES

✔ Participants will explore the ways in which poverty affects virtually all aspects of a person's life, including his or her health, education, human rights, and mortality.

✔ Participants will examine the cyclical nature of poverty.

Activity #1: What Is Poverty? (20 minutes)

Write one of the following questions on the board:

- *What do you think of when you hear the word "poverty"?*
- *What does poverty look like?*

Give participants five minutes to respond in writing. Next, give them a few minutes to share their answers with a partner. Then ask a few participants to share their thoughts with the group.

In discussing their thoughts you may wish to start with a dictionary definition of the word "poverty":

"Deficiency in amount or a lack in a means by which to provide for one's material needs or comfort. The condition of being poor." – The American Heritage Desk Dictionary

Using this definition, ask participants if they have ever seen poverty or if they know a very poor person or family. Have them explain. Also, what do they consider to be one's material needs?

 Note: Although most often people think of economic issues when they think of poverty, sometimes poverty is used to simply refer to a "lack of"—for example, poverty of the soul, poverty of morality, or poverty of culture. Nevertheless, for our purposes it is economic poverty that exists in the lives of nearly one-third of the world's people that is our concern.

Another matter that you might try to make clear here is that experts who study poverty describe at least two major kinds of poverty: "relative poverty" and "extreme poverty."

Relative Poverty

This means when compared to people or families around you, you are far poorer than they are, so relative to them, you are poor, but in an absolute sense, you may not be that poor at all.

Extreme Poverty

This kind of poverty is mostly found in some of the poorest countries in the world and often includes those people and families around the world who live on less than a dollar a day. Believe it or not, about one-sixth of the world's population, or almost 1.2 billion people, lives on less than a dollar a day. This kind of poverty affects most aspects of their lives and places them at a great risk since if their very small incomes are disrupted for even a few days or weeks by famine, war, illness, abuse, injustice, and even the loss of a family member or livestock, these individuals or their families can perish. It is the worst kind of poverty. For a quick overview on some poverty-related statistics, see **Handout 6-A**.

Activity #2: The Forgotten International's "Living on a Dollar a Day" (20 minutes)

After some discussion above, show participants the trailer to the TFI documentary **Living on a Dollar a Day** (4 minutes) twice. **www.theforgottenintl.org/build-awareness/living-on-a-dollar-a-day-the-documentary**. The first time, ask participants to write down images or words that stood out to them. Have participants share out images. This can be done as a "popcorn" call out, where participants volunteer answers without any feedback. This method keeps the flow empathic without initial intellectualization.

Now watch the video a second time, this time asking participants to pay attention to the narrative. Afterward, have them write two to four sentences explaining what they believe is the overall message of the video. Discuss this as a group, having participants share out their interpretations. Do they agree with the message of the trailer?

Also, after seeing this video, are there things that can be noted that make poverty, as seen in many parts of the world, different from the poverty that can be found here in the United States? Are there similarities?

Activity #3: Brainstorm Poverty Sorting (time varies)

Here, in a facilitator-directed brainstorm, ask participants to list the different aspects of a person's life affected by wealth. The categories the facilitator will likely end up with are health, health care, life expectancy, education, nutrition, shelter, friends, aspirations and opportunities, and possibly legal rights.

Then discuss with participants how and to what extent do they believe these aspects of one's life are negatively affected by poverty. In an effort to help them or bring some reality to this discussion, check out the Poverty Program website: **www.povertyprogram.com/statistics. php**.

Also, you could have participants sort through the statistics on this website and decide whether they are a cause or effect of poverty. For example, is the fact that very few impoverished girls finish school a cause of poverty or an effect of poverty? Participants will most likely struggle with this and have different answers. If you notice they are putting everything under the "effect" category, then push them to think about how lack of education might lead to poverty (i.e., lack of skills/literacy = unemployment/low-paying jobs, etc.). Afterward, discuss the results. This is a great exercise for helping to come to some understanding about what's been called "a cycle of poverty." As another example, the high percentage of mothers who die in childbirth is both a cause of poverty, since children will grow up as orphans, and an effect of poverty, because the mother didn't have the funds necessary to access needed health care.

Activity #4: "Help a Child" Role-Play (15 minutes)

Give each participant a card with the life scenario of an individual child. Example: Suhaeli is a young girl from Indonesia who wants to be an English teacher when she grows up. She is very hardworking and smart. She lives in a small village with her mother, who makes a dollar a day. The village school is very underfunded and overcrowded, and none of her teachers speak English. School is only free until sixth grade, and her mom doesn't have the money to send her on to middle school or beyond.

Give each participant a sheet of paper that looks like a path. At the beginning of the path, put Suhaeli's name (or the name of any other child being discussed) and at the end of the path put his or her dream. Have the participants brainstorm obstacles that the child will face in life that will hinder his or her ability to achieve her goals. See **Handout 6-B**.

To further expand on this activity, have participants get into groups based on their child's name (i.e., all participants who have Suhaeli come together). As a group, the participants are told they have inherited a combined $2,000 and free international airline tickets. It is their job to figure out how they can utilize their resources in order to help Suhaeli achieve her goal. This may include researching related nonprofit organizations or possibly brainstorm fundraising ideas in order to give Suhaeli a better chance at her dreams.

Activity #5: My Path (5 minutes)

Give participants a second "Path" paper (see **Handout 6-C**). Have participants put their name on one end and their dream on the other. Have them do the same exercise for themselves, except instead of obstacles, write the benefits they have that will help them get to their dreams. What do they have going for them to help them achieve their goals? Who helps them along the path? If they do have significant obstacles, they can put them there as well. This is a great way to circle back around to Lesson One on gratitude, as it is another way for participants to take note of their privileges and all the support they have in life.

Activity #6: Homework Ideas

• Have participants write a reflection on their "Help a Child" experience, explaining how they used the money and what insights they learned from the process.

• Have participants do research on organizations doing effective work to help fight poverty, and write a report about one such organization.

Handouts Lesson Six: Poverty Near and Far

Handout 6-A
Ten Facts on Global Poverty and Its Consequences

Handout 6-B
Path of Challenges

Handout 6-C
Path of Benefits

Handout 6-A: Ten Facts on Global Poverty and Its Consequences

1. Almost half the world, over three billion people, lives on less than $2.50 a day.

2. Almost 19,000 children under the age of five die every day due to circumstances related to poverty.

3. Nearly a billion people have entered into the 21st century unable to read a book or sign their names.

4. Millions of women around the world spend several hours each day going to collect water for themselves and their family's survival due to the fact that 1.1 billion people in developing countries have inadequate access to water.

5. Nearly a quarter of the world's population—1.6 billion people—live without any electricity.

6. At least 80% of people around the world live on less than $10 a day.

7. Less than 1% of what the world spends every year on weapons could make it possible for all children presently not attending school to receive an education.

8. Every year about 350–500 million people get malaria. Of those who die from the illness, 90% of those deaths occur in Africa, largely due to the fact that the poor either cannot afford health care or have no way of getting to a medical clinic.

9. Around the world nearly 40 million people are living with HIV/AIDS and over the last 35 years, 15 million children have lost one or both parents to this disease.

10. Over 790 million people in the developing world are chronically undernourished; two-thirds of these people reside in Asia and the South Pacific.

Handout 6-B: Path of Challenges

Child's Name _____

List of Obstacles

Obstacle 1

Obstacle 2

Obstacle 3

Obstacle 4

Obstacle 5

Obstacle 6

Child's Dream

Handout 6-C: Path of Benefits

Child's Name _____

List of Benefits

Benefit 1

Benefit 2

Benefit 3

Benefit 4

Benefit 5

Benefit 6

Child's Dream

Lesson Seven:
Out of Poverty

Basic Health Care | A Good Education | Job Opportunities

" Overcoming poverty is not a task of charity; it is an act of justice. Like slavery and apartheid, poverty is not natural. It is man-made and it can be overcome and eradicated by the actions of human beings. Sometimes it falls on a generation to be great. YOU can be that great generation. Let your greatness blossom. "

~ *Nelson Mandela*

Who Was Nelson Mandela?

Nelson Mandela was a South African social activist who fought to end apartheid through peaceful, nonviolent protests. In 1963 he was arrested, charged with treason, and imprisoned for 27 years. Mandela won the Nobel Peace Prize in 1993 for his work in dismantling apartheid and became the first African president of South Africa when he was elected in 1994.

LESSON SEVEN: PRINCIPAL OBJECTIVE

I n this lesson, we will attempt to explore several issues or questions with participants that are all related to giving as well as to assisting those in financial need. In doing so, we will try to address questions about what causes poverty and some of the ways we can help lift people out of poverty.

ADDITIONAL OBJECTIVES

✔ To demonstrate how compassionate acts can work to combat poverty and change lives.

✔ To show participants examples of how people have pulled themselves out of poverty through courage and resolve.

✔ To get participants to start thinking about ways in which they can get involved in alleviating poverty. In other words, create within them "a call to action!"

Activity #1: Some Words from Warren Buffett (10 minutes)

In 2007, former president Bill Clinton published a book called *Giving*. In it President Clinton wrote about a question he posed to Warren Buffett, one of the wealthiest individuals in the world. In short, the president asked Mr. Buffett why and how he came to the decision to give away $30 billion of his fortune to the Bill and Melinda Gates Foundation. (It was and remains the single largest personal charitable gift ever made. These funds will be used in the future to help some of the poorest people in the world.) To this question Mr. Buffett replied:

> "I could live very comfortably on less than 1% of that which I possess, all the rest is surplus. I have been lucky. I was born at the right time, in the right country, and have been disproportionately rewarded for the work I have done. It's the teachers, policemen and firemen who are our true heroes, and those who give up an evening out, or a dinner at a restaurant in order to be able to help others. I have given away nothing that I need, so please don't make of me a hero."

Read the story above about former President Clinton's question to Warren Buffett to the participants in the class and ask them for their thoughts on Mr. Buffett's answer. What are the key points that Mr. Buffett seems to be making?

Participants should point out at least three things:

1. That Mr. Buffett seems to acknowledge that the very wealthy have far more money than they need and, hence, giving away what is not needed is not necessarily a particularly heroic act.

2. That much of his wealth has not necessarily come from genius or any extraordinary talent. He just happened to be lucky and was disproportionately rewarded for what he has done. It's hard to say, but it's likely few very wealthy people would feel the same

way. Clearly, though, what Mr. Buffett states is likely true. He is nevertheless quite humble in recognizing and admitting this truth.

3. With the above in mind, Mr. Buffett refuses to be considered a hero, for in spite of giving away so much, he sacrificed nothing, unlike others who sacrifice much in order to help others.

To what extent do participants agree with Mr. Buffett?

Activity #2: Video "Feeding the Hungry, Nourishing the Soul" (10–15 minutes)

Watch this video about CNN Hero Narayanan Krishnan. (3 minutes)
www.youtube.com/watch?v=ZiC_9RHTvsA

How is the work that Narayanan Krishnan does different from Warren Buffett's? Please take note of how Mr. Krishnan seems to care about the nature of humanity, about the value of every human being, and how much he has given up to serve others. Who is doing more good? How are their messages different?

> **Note:** It is important that participants are not left with the impression that eradicating poverty is always about the "strong" helping the "weak."
>
> The video **"Back on My Feet"** does a good job at demonstrating how true change often comes from the empowerment of the impoverished. Watch the **"Back on My Feet"** video (5 minutes) **http://vimeo.com/38675251**

Activity #3: What Causes Poverty? (10–15 minutes)

Here, facilitators should go to the board and write the question, *"What causes poverty?"* Ask participants to try to think globally and allow them to shout out their answers. Write their answers on the board. Do not discuss what is suggested until all have had an opportunity to answer. Then cross out redundancy, if any, and propose a final list. See how close the participants lists come to that which is provided here. See **Handout 7-A**.

Activity #4: Ways to Help (20 minutes)

After participants have explored some of the causes of poverty, ask them to come up with ways to help the many millions around the world who live in poverty. Something you might suggest is that they simply take their list of causes of poverty and create a reverse action plan to address each of the causes they have on their list. For example, if we know that those around the world who are illiterate and have never attended school are far more likely to grow up poor and live a life of poverty, then one way to combat poverty is to enroll all youth in schools and provide them with programs to keep them there and help them get the skills in life they need. Theoretically, could such a list work as a starting point to help change the world? What would the biggest challenges be?

At the end of this discussion, have participants create a "How to Fix Poverty" poster. See **Handout 7-A** again for some hints as to what may or may not appear on their list.

Activity #5: Brainstorm, Reflect, and Plan (15 minutes)

In addition to Activity #4 or as an alternative activity, have participants talk about any initiatives or campaigns they know about that are devoted to helping the poor. Show them examples of how young people are giving. Challenge them to start thinking about projects they personally could do. For examples, see **Handout 7-B**.

Activity #6: Homework Idea

Have participants come up with a list of the most charitable people in history and explain why they put them on their list. Are there different ways to be charitable?

Handouts Lesson Seven: Out of Poverty

Handout 7-A
Twelve Causes of Poverty

Handout 7-B
Ten Things That, If Done, Would Help the World's Poor

Handout 7-A: Twelve Causes of Poverty

1. Overpopulation: It is in places in the world where there are large numbers of people and too little space, with few resources, that one is more likely to find poverty. This is not always the case, however, for although you will find a great deal of poverty in Bangladesh, one of the most densely populated countries in the world, some densely populated countries, such as the Netherlands and Belgium, have relatively little poverty. Nevertheless, it is still very true that overpopulation and population density play a role in poverty.

2. A Lack of Education: Education plays a large role in who will be literate, who will have the skills they need to find employment, and who may actually go on to higher education and achieve some wealth. With little education or substandard education, the chances of living in poverty increase dramatically. This is true all over the world, including the United States.

3. Environmental Degradation: In places in the world where the environment has been stripped of resources, and people have no means to farm or reap the benefits of what the earth produces for either personal consumption or sale at the marketplace, there is simply not enough around them that can drive their economy. As a result, they often grow up and live in poverty.

4. Changing Economic Trends: When people can't keep up with changing economic trends, often because they are unable to acquire the skills necessary to pursue evolving opportunities, they get left behind. Without governmental assistance or any community programs to aid them, they can fall into poverty.

5. Inadequate Infrastructure: Areas of the world that are remote, have few roads, rivers, airports, or are surrounded by natural barriers that make it difficult for trade to enter that region, often have high levels of poverty. The truth is that trade with others, either regionally or around the world, has done much to improve the standard of living of people throughout the planet. Impediments that make trade difficult often keep people in poverty.

6. Government Corruption: Governments that take money from their citizenry that otherwise would be going toward the needs of the poor or to development projects will keep a large segment of their population in poverty.

7. Discrimination: Some governments, companies, and individuals will, without much forethought, discriminate against certain people. Sometimes these are people who are thought to be of a lower caste or class, or maybe of a different religion or ethnic group, or may have a disability of some kind, or are of a gender that is not preferred. Nevertheless, for one reason or another, these people are marginalized and, as a result, are often cut off from opportunities offered to others and forced to live in poverty.

8. An Act of Nature: Sometimes people are driven into poverty through natural disasters. This may come as the result of a famine, a flood, or some horrific disease. These disasters can change people's lives by taking away the family's breadwinner or the land that nurtures them or, in some other way, their source of income. It may also displace them from a land they

Continued on next page

are familiar with, and, as a result, they may become refugees in a land that has no means to support them. All this can happen over the course of a day; no one ever knows who might end up in this kind of poverty.

9. War: In the same way a natural disaster may take over one's life and source of income, war or some kind of conflict can kill off family members, make it difficult to travel and participate in trade, or simply get to a place of employment. It, too, can force people to leave their community and be sent off to a place unknown with no means of support. Some of the poorest people in the world live in refugee camps all around the world and have been there for years.

10. A Failure to Provide for Themselves: Sometimes the poor throughout the world are, for one reason or another, unable to provide for themselves. They may be addicted to drugs or alcohol, or have other kinds of addictive behaviors that make it difficult for them to work or even plan for the future. They live day to day, and in some cases they may get help from family or the government, but, in other cases, they just survive. Employment is difficult, if not impossible, for in many cases the real problem is related to mental health issues or deficiencies that are often very difficult to treat, particularly on a large scale.

11. Poor Governance or the Lack of Compassion on the Part of Government: If one considers it the government's responsibility to take care of its people, then when a government fails in that role, it's people who suffer. Sometimes this means that the government has failed to protect the poor from exploitive practices on the part of unscrupulous employers. It may have failed to pass regulations that might protect its citizenry from economic downturn or laws that might better guard against greed or unfair business practices. Another possibility is that the government may have failed to distribute the nation's resources in a just and equitable manner or failed to provide any kind of governmental assistance to the poor or assist organizations that work to help the poor and empower them to help themselves. Finally, some government leaders may have failed, for one reason or another, to have compassion for those with little power, few skills, and no resources.

12. Demographic Shifts: Sometimes changes in the demographics of a particular country may bring about an increased level of poverty. For example, more and more families may decide they are no longer socially obligated to care for elderly family members, or couples may no longer remain married and decide it is acceptable to leave their children without providing them with adequate support. Another example of this would be if large numbers of people emigrated from rural communities into urban centers anticipating job opportunities only to find that there were none. This type of situation generally results in a great deal of dislocation, loss, and poverty.

Handout 7-B: Ten Things That, If Done, Would Help the World's Poor

1. Provide for more programs that improve the health of the poor.

2. Build more schools and provide for more educational and skill-based programs, particularly for impoverished young girls and women.

3. Support projects in poor countries that improve infrastructure, commerce, and roads.

4. Support programs that further new technologies and scientific advancements.

5. Support programs that encourage good governance and combat corruption.

6. Encourage governments to provide for safety net programs for the poor.

7. Encourage simple acts of kindness that help the poor by individuals, institutions, social groups, and faith communities.

8. Establish laws that further the advancement of programs that transfer wealth, for example progressive taxes, tax relief for charitable giving, and micro-loans to the poor.

9. Establish programs that encourage corporations to give back to the community and not exploit the poor and/or their labor force.

10. Pass laws protecting workers and set a minimum wage for those corporations that can't otherwise be encouraged.

Lesson Eight:
Needs, Wants, and Waste

" There's enough on this planet for everyone's needs but not for everyone's greed. **"**

~ Mahatma Gandhi

Who Was Mahatma Gandhi?

Mahatma Gandhi was the leader of India's independence movement from British rule and is most known for pioneering "Satyagraha," or resistance through mass nonviolent civil disobedience. To this day, Mahatma Gandhi's philosophies on nonviolent protests and simple living remain a great influence on oppressed and marginalized people throughout the world.

LESSON EIGHT: PRINCIPAL OBJECTIVE

This lesson poses some questions about how we in the United States, and to a lesser extent those in the developed world, might reconsider how we move through life, often consuming far more than we need only because we seem to have developed a habit of doing so or believe that more is better. This lesson hopes to help participants distinguish between their wants and their needs and identify some of the problems related to overconsumption.

ADDITIONAL OBJECTIVES

✔ Participants will be introduced to other societies and how they approach life and the acquisition of goods.

✔ Participants will question whether the acquisition of material goods has any relationship to happiness.

✔ Participants will watch **"Story of Stuff"** and create informational posters that examine one of the five links in the chain of consumption.

✔ Participants will begin to get a sense of the waste that is created by overconsumption.

 Note: America today, largely because of its "high standard of living" uses nearly 40% of that which is taken from the Earth in natural resources each year to provide for about 6% of the world's people. Hence, it can be said that we have a huge appetite for that which feeds our way of life, and we may be taking more than our fair share. In doing so, we leave quite a large environmental footprint.

Activity #1: What I Have, What I Want, and What I Need
(20 minutes)

Put participants into small groups and give each group a piece of butcher paper as well as a stack of sticky notes. Have them draw a line down the middle of the paper, labeling the left side "Have / Want" and the right side "Need." Then have them brainstorm the different things they own, as well as the things they want (examples: an iPhone, eight pairs of Nikes, a vacation home in Hawaii, etc.). Have them include the food they ate that day and what they'll eat that night. Have them write each item down on a separate sticky note (color-code based on whether it is a "have" or "want"), and then place them on one side of the sheet of butcher paper labeled "Have/Want."

Next, lead a discussion with participants about the idea of basic needs. What do people need to survive in life? (Examples: food, shelter, love/community, clothing, health, education.) Have participants look at their butcher paper full of sticky notes and have them move all of the basic needs over to the half of their sheet of butcher paper titled "Needs." What they will see is that the vast majority of the things they have on their notes are superfluous. Reflect on this with the participants.

Next, perhaps ask participants to expand from basic needs to "what do you need to be happy?" This can be a brief partner-share or informal full-class brainstorm session. This leads to interesting conversations, as participants will have differing opinions.

Next, present the group with a case study of a young person in a developing country. Perhaps he or she is an orphan, has AIDS, or is a young person laboring in a factory rather than going to school. Use examples of real people. Some photographs might be helpful. Then as a group discuss the "Needs" and "Haves" of this person. Have them compare and contrast themselves to this youth. They should recognize that the needs for survival are universal, but what people have and don't have are so different.

Activity #2: Video "Story of Stuff" and Poster Project
(30 minutes)

Divide the class equally into groups and designate each group as a link in the chain of stuff. There should be five groups (extraction, production, distribution, consumption, and disposal).

Have each group watch the entire 20-minute video of **"Story of Stuff"** <u>**www.storyofstuff.org/**</u> <u>**movies/story-of-stuff**</u>, but tell them they need to focus specifically on whichever of the five stages they have been assigned, taking notes on that part of the process and extracting the most compelling statistics.

Next, each group will create an informational poster or do a presentation about their designated stage, which includes an explanation, key statistics, harm caused, etc. If they prepare posters, have each group present their posters and then line them up on the wall in the appropriate sequence with arrows between. The last poster will be a class brainstorm of solutions and improvements. This way, not only will the participants in the various groups be experts, but everyone who might come to see these presentations will learn more about the story of stuff.

DEBRIEF:

When debriefing this day's activity, be sure to ask participants what they learned and what, if anything, surprised them about this lesson. Are they planning to share any of this information with friends? Will it affect the way they might behave as consumers in the future?

> **Note:** The poster activity may need to done as homework and then revisited at the beginning of the next class. Moreover, if time is short, you might consider just watching this video with the group and discussing some relevant questions. See **Handout 8-A**.

Handouts Lesson Eight: Needs, Wants, and Waste

Handout 8-A
Discussion Questions for "Story of Stuff"

Handout 8-A: Discussion Questions for "Story of Stuff"

Watch the video "Story of Stuff" and review the questions below for discussion with the group. You can have participants write down their answers first, or you can discuss the questions all together and note the responses on the board.

1. What do you think would be a good definition of "stuff"?

_____

_____

2. What are five things that you or your family have purchased recently that you would consider stuff?

_____

_____

3. Can you give an example of a product you own that has a "planned obsolescence"?

_____

_____

4. Can you give an example of a product you own that has a "perceived obsolescence"?

_____

_____

5. If it's true that those of us who live in the United States purchase more stuff (per capita) than people in any other country in the world, why might you think that is true? Give three reasons.

_____

_____

Continued on next page

6. Give three good reasons for reducing the amount of stuff people ordinarily buy. What might be three of the negative effects related to the acquisition of more and more stuff?

_____

_____

7. Are there positive consequences of acquiring more and more stuff? If so, what might they be? Are they sustainable?

_____

_____

8. Which stage of the extraction/production/consumption cycle in the making of stuff do you think needs to be fixed the most?

_____

_____

9. Are there statements made in this video that you would like to fact check and possibly do a report on in your class? If so, which ones?

_____

_____

10. Who do you think benefits the most from our current extraction/production/consumption system? Who suffers the most?

_____

_____

Continued on next page

Handout 8-A—Continued from previous page:
Discussion Questions for "Story of Stuff"

11. Did this video appear too one-sided, or do you think it is a truthful representation of how our world really works?

_____

_____

12. The video was made in 2007; do you think we are moving in the right direction, according to the presenter?

_____

_____

13. How did you feel after watching the video? Are you hopeful that we are making positive changes or depressed that it all seems the same?

_____

_____

14. Can you make a list of potential obstacles one might face in attempting to change the current wasteful system?

_____

_____

15. Did the video make you think about your personal shopping habits and those of your family? Are there consumer habits you would consider changing in your own life or suggest to your family after viewing "Story of Stuff"?

_____

_____

Continued on next page

HANDOUT 8-A 3 / 4

Handout 8-A—Continued from previous page:
Discussion Questions for "Story of Stuff"

16. Do you think advertising has affected the way you think of yourself or your self-esteem?

_____

_____

17. Do you agree with the presenter that companies try to make us buy things so we can feel happy? Do you think there's a link between happiness and consumerism? How long do you feel happy after you buy something you want? A day? A week? A month?

_____

_____

18. If you want to be a mindful consumer, what information would you like a company to share with you before you decide to buy their product?

_____

_____

19. Make a list of ways that corporations can make a more positive contribution to the planet. Can you name one company that today works to build a more sustainable planet?

_____

_____

20. Can you think of a class project whereby you might be able to share what you learned with others at your school to encourage them to rethink their buying practices?

_____

_____

Lesson Nine: Happiness

❝ Those who are happiest are those
who do the most for others. **❞**

~ *Booker T. Washington*

Who Was Booker T. Washington?

Booker T. Washington was one of the earliest African American civil rights leaders in U.S. history. Although born into slavery, Washington became an educated man through his hard work and determination. He put himself through school and in 1881 founded the Tuskegee Normal and Industrial Institute, which focused on educating and training African Americans in agricultural pursuits. Washington was the first African American to be invited to the White House and also served as an adviser to President Theodore Roosevelt.

LESSON NINE: PRINCIPAL OBJECTIVE

I n this lesson, we will attempt to sort out those things that truly make people happy from those things that do not, and share with participants some of the recent science that has gone into the study of happiness as well as our pursuit of happiness. Too many people believe that wealth and the acquisition of material goods have a direct impact on one's happiness. The truth is that such correlations are at best, minimal, or may not exist at all. Nevertheless, it's a myth that we should address in this course while at the same time reminding participants of some of the most effective ways to live a happier life, one of which is by demonstrating kindness and generosity toward others.

ADDITIONAL OBJECTIVES

✔ Participants will measure their own Happiness IQs and contemplate what makes them happy in life.

✔ Participants will discover key facts and concepts about happiness through the documentary *Happy.*

✔ Participants will discuss and work with others in order to identify and articulate some keys to happiness.

Activity #1: What Makes People Happy? Write-Pair-Share

(10–15 minutes)

Put the question *"What makes people happy?"* on the board. Give participants three minutes to think and write their answer. Then have them discuss their opinions with each other. As a group, have participants share their opinions. Make a list of their thoughts on the board.

Activity #2: Your Happiness IQ (10 minutes)

There are a number of "happiness tests" online that would be interesting for participants to take. Some of them are quite involved.

One is quite simple and fun. It only has five questions. Have participants take out a sheet of paper and answer the questions as you read the questions out loud. For the simple Answer Key, see **Handout 9-A**.

Happiness Quiz

1. What is more powerful?

    Smiles

    Chocolate bars

2. Yoga is an exercise that can make you feel good. This exercise originated in what country?

    China

    India

    Japan

    Yoga-slavia

3. Which can help your mood?

    Music

    Smell

    Sleep

    All of the above

4. Richer people are happier?

    True

    False

5. Which food will best put you in a good mood?

    Ice cream

    Avocado

    Cheese

    Apple

For the web version of a similar quiz, see **www.webmd.com/balance/rm-quiz-happiness**.

Activity #3: What Makes YOU Happy? Top Ten List (10–15 minutes)

Have each participant make a list of ten things that make them happy. They can refer back to the opening brainstorming session if they like.

Discuss with them the difference between "short-term" and "long-term" happiness—in other words, happiness that is fleeting versus a kind of happiness (or well-being) that may last a lifetime. Then have participants go through their lists (perhaps with a partner) and determine whether each thing that makes them happy is short-term or long-term. Example: A cold drink on a sunny day versus a family that loves you.

📽 Activity #4: Movie *Happy, a Documentary* (25 minutes)

This documentary is a wonderful way of opening up a serious discussion about what makes people happy. Since happiness is something we all strive for, it is clearly an important discussion to have with the participants in this program. This video can be watched either at home or in a group setting. Since it is a little longer than the group may have time for, we have broken it up as to the minutes you might watch that are most relevant to this course. Facilitators should, however, watch the entire film before going through it with the group in this manner. This video is not available on the web for free. You can, however, acquire it through Netflix or through **www.thehappymovie.com**. Again, here are the most revealing points to explore:

Minutes 14–16: Flow

This segment introduces the idea of flow—finding something we enjoy doing so much that it takes us to a state of flow—which is happiness. Of course, this may only be an example of short-term happiness or well-being, but nevertheless it does uplift us in ways that affect our mood and may make life easier.

Minutes 23–26: Dispels the Myth that Money Equals Happiness

Here the video shows that having enough money to lift oneself out of poverty and the struggles and stress that sometimes come with having little control over one's financial well-being increases happiness a great deal, but after that, there isn't any positive correlation between making more money and being happier. Once your basic needs are met, money no longer affects happiness. At that point, happiness comes from other sources. The film also discusses the hedonic treadmill, all done in an engaging way through graphs, interviews, and experts.

Minutes 28–30: Intrinsic Goals versus Extrinsic Goals

> **Extrinsic:** Image/status/popularity (you become less happy)

> **Intrinsic:** Personal growth/close relationships/helping others
>   (you become more happy)

Minutes 52–58: Competition versus Collaboration

This segment shows how people's natural tendency is to want to collaborate rather than compete. In other words, it makes us happier to work with people rather than against them. The film then shows a clip of a guest speaker at a middle school speaking on the themes of compassion, working together, and treating each other well. It's quite instructive.

Minute 102: Dalai Lama on Compassion

Here, the Dalai Lama talks about how compassion is our most natural instinct. That we know from birth that all we want is our mother, for nearly all mothers have immense compassion toward their children. Compassion makes both the recipient and the giver feel happier.

Minute 106: Altruism

Here, the film tells the story of a banker who leaves his job and moves to India and volunteers at Mother Teresa's Home for the Destitute and Dying. He talks about how happy he is there, how these moments of connection and giving give him so much more joy and peace than his previous life of money making.

Minutes 109–113: Final Conclusions

During the last few minutes of this film, the producers summarize all the key points of the movie and give the viewer their final insights.

Activity #5: Intrinsic versus Extrinsic Goals (12 minutes)

Have participants gather in groups and discuss and sort out intrinsic values (i.e., close relationships, gratitude, etc.) and extrinsic values (i.e., status, popularity, etc.); then explain what the difference is between the two groups. Which one is more likely to lead you to long-term happiness and why?

Activity #6: Take-Away Idea (optional)

Have each participant in the group explain what one part, one moment, or one person in the video struck them or stood out to them the most and why.

Activity #7: Happiness Top Five (15 minutes)

Divide participants into small groups and have each group create a top-five list of "Keys to Happiness." Have each small group present their lists to the full group. See if there are many items on the lists they all seem to agree on. Offer your own thoughts.

For a summary of many of the points made in this film as well as other thoughts that some have had about what makes us happy, see **Handout 9-B**, "Nine Keys to Happiness."

Activity #8: Movie *Pursuit of Happyness* (6 minutes)

Please consider having your group watch this clip from the movie "***Pursuit of Happyness - Ending Scene***" (4 minutes) **www.youtube.com/watch?v=pCq7eGKcs-w**. It's from the movie with Will Smith and shows how a previously homeless man finally gets a job and can now care for his son whom he loves dearly. In doing so, he's likely never been so happy. Have participants consider whether it is a job or money that has made him happy or something else. What is the relationship between money and happiness?

Activity #9: Homework Idea

Create a plan for yourself that works to increase happiness in your own life.

Handouts Lesson Nine: Happiness

Handout 9-A
Answer Sheet to Happiness Quiz

Handout 9-B
Nine Keys to Happiness

Handout 9-A: Answer Sheet to Happiness Quiz

1: What is more powerful?

A: Smiles. Smiles create a lot more happiness than chocolate. Yep, it's true. To get the same kind of happy feelings in your brain that one smile causes, you'd have to eat a lot of chocolate —2,000 bars! Who knew one smile could be so powerful? Plus, a smile is way better for you than lots of candy. Smiling and laughing make you feel good. Try it!

2: Yoga is an exercise that can make you feel good. This exercise originated in what country?

A: India. Yoga started in India more than 3,000 years ago. When you do yoga, you stretch, hold poses, and take deep breaths. If you're feeling bad, try reaching up and stretching really big. Gentle exercise like yoga can help your mood. Exercises like swimming or soccer can help, too. Moving helps your brain make chemicals that make you feel good. It doesn't matter how you move—when you move, it just feels good.

3: Which can help your mood?

A: All the Above. What you hear and smell can change your mood. But sleep makes a really big difference. If you don't get enough sleep just one night a week, it can make it hard to think. Being tired can make you stressed, angry, and sad too. When you sleep enough, you feel good. When you're well rested, you'll have energy to move, play, or exercise.

4: Richer people are happier?

A. False. Money is not the way to find happiness. As long as people have a home and food, lots of money doesn't make them happier. What does make people happier? Try spending time with friends, family, or teammates. People are social animals, and as such, these kinds of loving relations help one's mood in a positive way.

5: Which food will best put you in a good mood?

A. Avocados. The green avocado has good mood powers. Its secret is its omega-3 fatty acids. These healthy fats can help keep your heart healthy and boost your mood.

Handout 9-B: Nine Keys to Happiness

1. Give yourself permission to be human: Remember we all make mistakes, and we cannot be all things to all people. You must forgive yourself as you forgive others. To not forgive only forces you to harbor anger or ill feelings, none of which leads to happiness.

2. Pleasure and meaning: It has been said that happiness lies at the intersection of pleasure and meaning. There is some truth to this. Think of the times when you did something that was both pleasurable and meaningful, for example, having a great day with someone you love, winning a big game, your graduation from high school or college, or that day you helped someone in desperate need, and but for you, a tragedy was averted. All are examples of brief moments of joy and happiness; nevertheless, all are quite powerful, and if you sprinkle your life with such occurrences as often as possible, you will indeed create for yourself a very happy life.

3. Money and your state of mind: Happiness is mostly dependent on your state of mind, not on the state of your bank account. Certainly economic security relieves stress, and no one wants to worry about whether they will be able to feed their family or pay the rent. The trick is to keep your life simple, explore everything in moderation, and manage your affairs. Once your needs and those of your loved ones are in order, then you can focus on your attitude and approach to life. In doing so, always try to remain kind, positive, and optimistic. When you interact with life in this manner, good things happen.

4. Count your blessings: There are few things in life that we are entitled to, hence most of what we receive should be thought of as gifts. Whether it's a sunny day, a warm smile from a stranger, a phone call from a friend you have not heard from in some time, or simply another day to appreciate being alive, you should be thankful. If you go through life with this attitude, it is easier to feel fortunate and you are less likely to feel cheated, frustrated, jealous, or angry about something you did not receive. These kinds of emotions only detract from happiness. So again, it's your attitude and approach to life that's very important.

5. Remember the mind-body connection: Take care, exercise, eat right, and remain in touch with your body and mind. Few would disagree that being as healthy as possible has a direct relationship with what you can and cannot do and how you experience the world and all those who are important in your life. It's important also to try to alleviate stress, and one way of doing that is by remaining active and healthy.

6. Work at something you love: Work is such a big part of one's life. In fact, it often occupies the majority of one's waking hours. To choose a job or career that does not bring you some joy subtracts from the time you have in life to experience joy and happiness. Getting up and going to work should not be something you dread. Life is too short. Unfortunately, and as we all know, jobs that bring one joy are not always easy to come by. Nevertheless, we should see this as one of our goals in life, a goal to work toward. The first step in achieving that goal is to find out what your passion is, and then work backward to sort out the way to get there.

7. Avoid overattachment, dependence, or addictions: Life is ever-changing. Those who may be in your life one day, may be gone the next. Children grow up, jobs change, friends move or pass away. For those reasons it is important not to put all of your life's joys in the hands of other people, places,

Continued on next page

objects, or substances. To do so only risks great loss and sadness. Also, depending on others to safeguard your economic security or to bring you happiness is very dangerous for it leaves you at their whim, and before too long, you have lost control of your life. We must retain the ability to provide and protect ourselves. We must be able to brighten our own days, to be happy when we are all alone, and to sing, even when no one hears us. Of course, this sometimes is very difficult, for it is so easy to yearn for those we have grown close to. The trick is to learn to love your own company. Sometimes that's all we have.

8. Nurture your relationships: In spite of what has been said above, no one can deny that human beings are social animals. We receive much pleasure through our relationships with others, whether they be family, friends, or lovers. It is more difficult to be happy if you have no one in your life, and in fact, many have said that happiness is best when it is shared. With this in mind, spend some time developing friendships and keeping those you care for involved in your life.

9. Plan for the future: The notion of planning for the future and its relationship to happiness has been met with some skepticism. In fact, some would say that putting too much time and effort into what tomorrow may bring not only may be a waste of time but also may detract from one's ability to "live in the moment." Certainly, it doesn't make sense to spoil your ability to enjoy today with worries about tomorrow, particularly when those concerns are about something you may not be able to change. Hence, to at least this extent, "living in the moment" is very important. Nevertheless, this does not mean that you should not plan for the future. The truth is that most of us will live a long life, and it is in living your life that you will learn what brings you joy. So whether it's family, friends, your work, a safe place to live, or simply some time to read, travel, help others, or play, make sure that these aspects of life will be available to you as you transition from your youth to your old age. This requires planning and sometimes advice from others. Don't forget to take care of this while you are young. Too many of the world's elderly never planned for their future and end up forgotten with little joy in their lives. Don't let this happen to you.

An additional note about the relationship between wealth and happiness:

Over the years many studies have been done on the relationship between wealth, or the acquisition of material goods, and happiness. Most studies have found that although there are some correlations, the relationship is at best, weak. There are two things, however, that these studies have discovered:

One: If the elements that go into the making of happiness were divided up into two categories, the first being social values (namely, love, family, and friends) and the second being material values (economic security and "success"), the former outranks the latter in terms of importance. This is not to say that one's economic security is not important, but above a certain level of income and comfort, material things seem to stop giving us the kind of satisfaction that the material world would sometimes like us to believe.

Continued on next page

Handout 9-B—Continued from previous page:
Nine Keys to Happiness

Two: When people have been asked what makes them happy, they have said what they really want out of life is autonomy and control over their life, good self-esteem, warm family relationships, tension-free days, leisure time, close and intimate friends, as well as romance and love. So when pursuing happiness in life, be sure to think hard about the choices you make.

Finally, remember there are few lives that have been lived long that have not experienced some disappointment, sadness, sorrow, and even suffering. The above is not meant as an attempt to immunize one from such human experiences, but only to lessen them in frequency and severity. The good news is that we can all learn from difficult times and become stronger and smarter for them, and it's because of the rainy days that we appreciate the sunny days all the more.

Lesson Ten: Doing Good

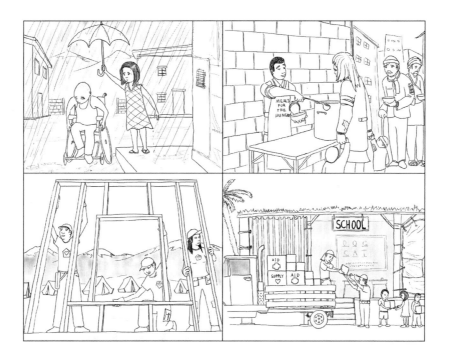

" Never doubt that a small group of thoughtful, committed citizens can change the world. Indeed, it is the only thing that ever has. **"**

~ Margaret Mead

Who Was Margaret Mead?

Margaret Mead was a celebrated American anthropologist, author, and educator who is credited with making the field of anthropology (the study of humans, their customs, and behaviors) accessible to the wider public. Her most famous work focused on attitudes toward sex in far-removed South Pacific and Southeast Asian cultures, as well as studies of these cultures after experiencing extended exposure to the wider world.

LESSON TEN: PRINCIPAL OBJECTIVE

This lesson is about "doing good" and although the emphasis of this lesson is on the word "doing," the "good," of course, is the starting point and is very important, for one could spend a lifetime doing little (or worse, doing evil), and that is obviously not what our world needs. Remember, all of us are capable of choosing either path. Hopefully, however, after experiencing this program and being inspired by the words and deeds of those who have worked to make the world a better place, participants will choose the path of promise, of optimism, and of meaning and thereby work to do good, not only at the conclusion of this lesson and program but also throughout their lives. That is our hope, not only for participants but for all who have the ability to give and care for others.

ADDITIONAL OBJECTIVES

✔ Participants will contemplate what it means to be a good person and identify traits associated with goodness.

✔ Participants will review and attempt to encapsulate much of what they have learned over the course of the previous nine lessons in order to better prepare themselves to move forward with their work.

✔ Participants will begin to plan and eventually complete a project that will help others who may not have the same advantages as themselves.

 Note: In this final lesson, you should not try to limit yourself to the time it may take to complete a traditional class. In fact, it may take several "classes" to bring participants to a point where they will be ready to create a project that will benefit others as well as themselves. Also, time should be dedicated here to some kind of closure of the substantive aspect of this program, by way of a culminating assignment, a presentation, an opportunity to reflect on what has been learned, and/or a celebration. But remember, this final lesson should serve as a stepping stone into your action project. Hence, there is still a lot to do!

There are a variety of ways to bring this aspect of the lesson to a conclusion, and none are exclusive of others. However, at this point, it might make sense to make sure that by now there exists some consensus as to what is "good" or what it means to "be good," at least for purposes of this program and one's actions toward helping others.

Activity #1: What Makes a Person Good? Brainstorm and Discussion

Write on the board: *Who is someone in your life who you consider to be a "good" person? What makes him/her good?* Have participants write their answers to these two questions and then share them with a partner. Then draw a T-chart on the board with one column, "Good," and another column, "Bad." Then have participants brainstorm traits that good people have and traits that bad people have. Next, have them talk about people they consider "good" and see if they match the characteristics brainstormed by the class.

Activity #2: Doing Good in Hollywood

Ask participants: *What do Angelina Jolie, Kobe Bryant, and Lady Gaga have in common?*

Explain to them that what they have in common is that they spend a considerable amount of time giving and caring for others. You can search for other celebrities and the causes they support at "Look to the Stars: The World of Celebrity Giving": **https://www.looktothestars.org/**

Have participants get in partners and together chose a celebrity or a few celebrities from the list of celebrity philanthropists/activists. Have participants do further research on their chosen celebrities' actions that have demonstrated their desire to help others.

Activity #3: Homework Idea

As a possible homework assignment, have participants write a profile of a famous philanthropist who is not necessarily a celebrity and include such information as: How did they first get into philanthropy? How did they come to choose specific causes? Why do they feel it is important to give? How much time/money/energy do they devote to philanthropy?

In completing this assignment, hopefully participants will gain a deeper understanding of the whys of philanthropy, and come to the conclusion that the desire and commitment to share one's wealth and good fortune bring meaning to one's life.

DEBRIEF:

After students have examined the philanthropic side of Hollywood, pose questions to them such as: *Do you think that because people have the means, it is their responsibility to be philanthropists? Do you think it is appropriate and/or effective for public figures to use their popularity to draw attention to specific causes? If you are wealthy, are you obligated to give some of your money away?*

Activity #4: A Course Review

Another way to try to bring to a close this aspect of the program is to divide what the group has learned thus far into two branches of learning: that which has been character-based and that which has been knowledge-based. For example:

CHARACTER-BASED CONTENT

The cultivation and appreciation for:

- *Gratitude.* What specifically did you learn about yourself?
- *Empathy.* When did you feel what others may have felt?

- *Compassion.* Give an example of when you witnessed someone demonstrating compassion.
- *Happiness.* When are you most happy? Why?
- *Goodness.* Who do you know that is "good" and why?

KNOWLEDGE-BASED CONTENT

A better understanding of:

- *Some of our world's problems and challenges.*
- *What you learned about human diversity and an acknowledgement of our commonality and inter-connectedness.*
- *Some of the causes and consequences of poverty on a global scale.*
- *Whether you believe we have a tendency toward overconsumption. Can you distinguish between your needs and your wants?*

So now the question is: How do we create a lesson that challenges participants to reflect or articulate their understanding of these core concepts and facts about the world's challenges?

Here are some possible ideas and activities:

Activity #5: Develop (as a Group) a Website or Blog about the Course

This site might include, but is not limited to:

- Several pages about how have they practiced gratitude over the past 10 weeks—it can be in blog form and include anecdotes and pictures.
- Several pages about how they've practiced kindness over the past 10 weeks. Again, this can be in blog form and include examples.
- One page devoted to what has made them happy over the past 10 weeks, including perhaps how compassion and gratitude have played a part in feeling happy.
- A page about the world's problems and what needs to be fixed in the world.
- Some pages about poverty—the extent to which it exists in this world, the people affected, the various causes and effects of poverty.
- A page about the extent to which overconsumption affects the world we share.
- As a variation on this idea, you might even have the entire group start a blog together at the beginning of the course and add to it over the course of the program. On the last day the participants would design pages explaining what endeavors they plan to take on in the pursuit of helping others. This would include the cause and community served, as well as how they plan on helping their chosen community. They may even want to reflect on how they feel now about compassion and giving versus when they started this program.

Activity #6: Essay and Presentation

Have participants write an essay about how the course has changed their perspectives on the world and what is important in life. Give guidelines and requirements. Provide a way of sharing these essays. If time is short, perhaps just one or two of the essays might be read aloud to the group.

Activity #7: Reflection Circle

Take a fishbowl or a bag and put into it several folded sheets of paper that have questions having to do with gratitude, kindness, or happiness. For instance, "Name three things in this world that make you happy," "What is the kindest thing you did over the past 10 weeks?" or "Who is one person you are most grateful for and why?" Prior to starting the activity, have participants take a moment to think about how gratitude, kindness, and happiness have shown up in their lives over the past 10 weeks. Then put the participants in a circle and pass the fishbowl or bag around, with each participant arbitrarily picking and answering a question. At the end of this activity, have each participant create a poster with a top-ten list of the most important things they learned about life, the world, or themselves over the course of the program. Present or display the posters so they can share their list with each other and the world.

Now the Real Work Begins

In the first part of this program, participants have been examining what is truly important in life and brainstorming causes they believe might help to make the world a better place. Also, they have taken part in activities that have, hopefully, caused them to consider their aspirations in life, as well as what kind of role they might wish to play in the world around them. In this part of the program, they will narrow their focus to one cause or community and start planning and effectuate an initiative or project that will work to help others who have not had the same advantages they have had or may be struggling with challenges. Be sure to explain the next steps they will be taking.

THE STEPS IN THE PROCESS

1. Deciding on a person, group, or organization that will be helped

This decision should be made by all the participants at a group meeting. Participants should feel free to nominate a person in need, or a group, or an organization that works to help those in need. This person or group could be located in and around their local community, or located in another part of the world entirely. In fact, as has been suggested in this curriculum, it is in many ways more effective to help people abroad, for the resources you can provide them often go much farther in another country than here in the United States. Nevertheless, there are advantages to working locally, including a feeling that you can better get to know those you have helped if they are nearby. In coming to some decision, however, try to do so in a democratic fashion, and once a decision has been made, try to encourage everyone to be supportive of that decision, regardless of whether it was their first choice. Remember, this is about doing good, and not about ego. For some suggestions on what organizations you might look to for advice on how you might help others in need, see "National Organizations That Do Good" **(Appendix #9)**.

2. Begin to brainstorm ways in which to help

Once a person or organization has been chosen, the group then needs to turn its attention to figuring out exactly what they can do together to serve the individual or group in need. There is always a variety of things that you can do to help another, but you must keep in mind what is manageable within a specific time, and what most people are willing to work on together. It should, of course, be something that benefits the participants in some way as well, whether that be enhancing their organizational skills, or simply touching their heart in the act of doing and giving.

3. Set achievable goals

It is always important to set out a reasonable goal for yourself in the process of trying to help others (e.g., raise x amount of dollars to help support an orphanage abroad). Remember goals need to be set with your resources and timeline in mind. Setting goals too high creates frustration and a feeling of failure. Setting goals too low may in fact undermine all the good you are trying to do. So goals must be reasonable in light of resources, the energy people have, and the time constraints you might be under. You need to give all of this considerable thought. If you decide that the best way to help a person or organization is to simply raise some needed funds for them to, for example, pay for some school or medical supplies, or to install a water purification system, or build new classrooms, or even to donate food, shoes, or school supplies for impoverished children, see "Fundraising Ideas" **(Appendix #8)**.

4. Start putting together a plan for how they will achieve this goal

People always have good ideas ("let's do this," or "let's do that," or "let's try something else"), and often when there is a group discussion as to what could or should be done, there are individuals within the group who always seem to say, "No, we can't do that" or "That won't work." So instead of being optimistic and positive and willing to run with the energy and ideas people have, a lot of negativity often comes into the discussion. What you wish to do here, at least initially, is try to be open to any idea, and then try to find out how much support there is for that idea. As long as the time and energy is there, it might be worth trying. At the end of the discussion, put all of the good ideas you believe to be doable on the board and then try to shape that into a plan: what should be done first, second, and so on. Then begin the process of moving forward.

5. Assign group leaders, set timelines, and prepare to get to do the work of "Doing Good"

Another problem that often occurs when groups of individuals attempt to work together is what has been called a "diffusion of responsibility." This happens when too many people see themselves as being responsible for everything, and when something doesn't get done, they assume that someone else will take care of it. As a result, no one is responsible for any one goal or objective. Hence, the responsibility is diffused, and at the end of the day, little, if anything, gets done. So, in order to effectively move forward, you must assign specific tasks to specific people and create group leaders, or even committees, to work on specific tasks, with timelines as to when things need to be accomplished. Each person or committee should report any difficulties they are having in the hope that the group can help suggest solutions. Finally, you need one person who oversees everything and simply makes sure that people are doing what they are supposed to be doing in the right time, the right order, and in the right place, all with an eye on meeting the goals of the group, and eventually doing some good for those you have decided to help. All of this is not easy, but, in the end, all should rejoice in the satisfaction of making life better for someone or possibly many others.

Activity #8: Video "Pre-School Kindness" by RandomActsofKindness (3 minutes)

Finally, for those participants who believe that this is too much work or that they cannot possibly do anything of any significance to help others, they should watch the video **"Pre-School Kindness"** (3 minutes): **https://www.youtube.com/watch?v=JRaBKR6EKow**. It is quite heartwarming and brings home the lesson that nearly all of us can do something to help others.

It is now time to Do Good,
not only for the remainder of this program
or year but also for the rest of your life!
The truth is, the world needs you
and people like you.

Appendices 1–11:
Ideas & Resources

❝ I wish to do something Great and Wonderful, but I must start by doing the little things like they were Great and Wonderful. **❞**

~ Albert Einstein

Note: These Appendices will grow and change over the years and new resources will be added as the curriculum is used by more and more educators and facilitators. We hope you will contribute to these lists as you find related videos, projects, and websites to add.

Appendix #1: Ideas for Activities or for Use as Homework Assignments

- In the first class meeting, consider a bonding exercise of one kind or another.

- Students may want to create a simple a website or blog for the course.

- Have participants keep a gratitude or compassion journal in which they write about what they are learning, their responses to some of the questions posed in the lessons, their thoughts and emotions about global poverty issues, as well as any acts of kindness they perform over the course of the program.

- Have participants list the characteristics that they believe go into the making of a hero. Afterward, have them list heroes from throughout history to see if those people match up with the characteristics they have identified.

- Ask participants, if they were given $1,000 and told to give it all away, what would they do with it and why?

- Ask participants to perform small acts of kindness every day over the next week. How do they feel at the end of the week? What happened as a result of their efforts?

- Ask participants to role-play the part of a homeless person and while doing so have him/her interviewed by another participant. Alternatively, role-play someone who has lost everything in a devastating flood or fire, or in an earthquake or tornado.

- Have participants write a "A Day in the Life of _____" story. For example, a day in the life of a homeless teenager or a parent who is working multiple jobs for his/her family.

- Invite a guest speaker to address the group, such as a philanthropist or someone from a local nonprofit who works with the homeless or even a happiness expert, and have participants pose ten questions.

- Have participants count their blessings or make a list of what they are most grateful for. Ask them if they wish to share their list with others in the group.

- Distribute small candies or other sharable items to participants in the group based on the wealth of different countries around the world. For example, if you live in the United States, you have this much each day; if you live in Thailand, you live on this much; and if you live in Liberia, you only get this much. How do participants feel about how much they have? How do they feel about what others have in other countries?

- Have participants list what they believe are the world's biggest problems or challenges.

- Ask participants how the Golden Rule is portrayed in many of the world's religions. The Golden Rule, of course, is to "do unto others what you want others to do unto you."

- Ask participants, who are three people they admire most in history? Who are three people they least admire? Why do they think so?

- Have participants prepare a list of celebrities that do good. What kinds of charitable acts do they perform? Do famous people amplify charitable causes? Is that important?

- Brainstorm examples of kindness and unkindness, and talk about the consequences of each. How do you feel when you are supported? How do you feel when you are bullied? How do you feel when you are helping someone in need? How do you feel when you are putting someone down?

- Give participants examples of everyday heroes who do charitable work, including young people their age.

- Discuss the "Twelve Simple Beliefs" of The Forgotten International listed at the end of this curriculum, and have participants write a short paragraph on what each belief means to them. Do they agree or disagree with any of the beliefs?

- Do an exercise aimed at defining compassion. Share these definitions with other participants and discuss what might be different levels of compassion.

- Discuss what compassion looks like and why is it important.

- Define these terms: compassion, sympathy, pity. What is empathy or altruism or kindness? Can participants give examples of each?

- Write a biography of someone you consider a hero.

- Write a biography of a famous philanthropist. How did their charitable acts make a difference in the community?

- Have participants write a biography of one of their parents or grandparents. Conduct an interview to learn about their life.

- What are different ways of giving? Point out how much we all have to give—time, talent, treasure.

- Do an exercise aimed at defining "the common good." In other words, what is good for all is the common good. Put participants in groups of three (one takes notes), and have two rattle off what they have in common. Examples: all of us want to feel safe, we need shelter, love, education, belonging, friendship, etc. The purpose of this exercise is to demonstrate commonality between individuals, groups, and communities.

- List actions you have taken that have benefited the common good.

- Ask participants to define needs versus wants. Have them make a list of their needs and their wants; then have them break down their needs list further by selecting their most basic needs. What is the difference between a "need" and a "want"?

- Have participants write an "I am" poem from the perspective of someone else—for example, "I am homeless," "I am undocumented," "I am an orphan."

- Make use of Skype to connect with a classroom in another part of the world.

- Make an "If I Ruled the World" poster. What would I do? What would I change?

- View a compelling photo and describe what you see, feel, wish to know, and what you would do about what is portrayed in the photo. You could also write a story based on the photo and, in doing so, try to imagine the background of the person in the photo.

- Have participants prepare a presentation based on one of the books from the Suggested Readings list included as **Appendix #2.**

Appendix #2: Suggested Readings

1. *A Fearless Heart: How the Courage to Be Compassionate Can Transform Our Lives* (2015) – by Thupten Jinpa, PhD

The Buddhist practice of mindfulness caught on in the West when we began to understand the everyday, personal benefits it brought us. Now, in this extraordinary book, the highly acclaimed thought leader and longtime English translator of His Holiness the 14th Dalai Lama shows us that compassion can bring us even more. Based on the landmark course in compassion training Jinpa helped create at the Stanford School of Medicine, *A Fearless Heart* shows us that we actually fear compassion. We worry that if we are too compassionate with others, we will be taken advantage of, and if we are too compassionate with ourselves, we will turn into slackers. Using science, insights from classical Buddhist and Western psychology, and stories both from others and from his own extraordinary life, Jinpa shows us how to train our compassion muscle to relieve stress, fight depression, improve our health, achieve our goals, and change our world.

2. *Buy, Use, Toss? A Closer Look at the Things We Buy* (2010) – by Facing the Future (Curriculum)

Buy, Use, Toss? is a free interdisciplinary unit that includes ten fully planned lessons. This unit is correlated with national science and social studies standards and will lead your participants through an exploration of the system of producing and consuming goods that is called the materials economy.

3. *Choose the Life You Want: 101 Ways to Create Your Own Road to Happiness* (2012) – by Tal Ben-Shahar

Ben-Shahar shows how making the right choices—not the big, once-in-a-lifetime choices, but rather the countless small choices we make every day almost without noticing—has a direct, long-lasting impact on our happiness. Every single moment is an opportunity to make a conscious choice for a happy and fulfilled life. *Choose the Life You Want* covers 101 such choices, complete with real-life stories to help you identify and act on opportunities large and small.

4. *The Complete Guide to Service Learning: Proven, Practical Ways to Engage Students in Civic Responsibility, Academic Curriculum, & Social Action* (2nd ed. 2010) – by Cathryn Berger Kaye

This project-based guide is a blueprint for service learning—from getting started to assessing the experience—and integrates the K–12 Service-Learning Standards for Quality Practice. An award-winning treasury of activities, ideas, annotated book recommendations, author interview, and expert essays—all presented within a curriculum context and organized by theme.

5. *Everyday Heroes: 50 Americans Changing the World One Nonprofit at a Time* (2012) – by Katrina Fried

Two years ago, photographer Paul Mobley and author and editor Katrina Fried set out to find 50 Americans who had made it their business to improve the lives of others. The result is this groundbreaking book profiling some of America's leading social entrepreneurs, whose energy and nonprofit organizations have changed the lives of millions around the world, very often one at a time.

6. *40 Chances: Finding Hope in a Hungry World* (2014) – by Howard G. Buffett

A son of legendary investor and philanthropist Warren Buffett, Howard G. Buffett considers himself a farmer first and foremost. He explains that all farmers get 40 growing seasons in their lifetime, giving them just 40 chances to make a difference. Buffett describes his quest to help the most vulnerable people on earth—nearly a billion individuals who lack basic food security. The younger Buffett has focused his foundation on wildlife conservation and world hunger. *40 Chances: Finding Hope in a Hungry World* is a compelling look at Buffett's lessons learned as he seeks new approaches to ease the suffering of many.

7. *Giving: How Each of Us Can Change the World* (2007) – by Bill Clinton

Giving is an inspiring look at how each of us can change the world. It reveals the extraordinary and innovative efforts now being made by companies and organizations—and by individuals—to solve problems and save lives both "down the street and around the world." Then it urges us to seek out what each of us, regardless of income, age, and skills, can do to give people a chance to live out their dreams.

8. *Good Citizens: Creating Enlightened Society* (2012) – by Thich Nhat Hanh

Good Citizens is Zen Master Thich Nhat Hanh's bold contribution to the creation of a shared global ethic. Thich Nhat Hanh lays out a vision based on the Four Noble Truths that speak to people of all faiths, cultures, and political beliefs. If we understand them closely, they can be a guide to help us think, act, and speak in ways that bring more joy and peace to ourselves and others.

9. *Half the Sky: Turning Oppression into Opportunity for Women Worldwide* (2010) – by Nicholas Kristof and Sheryl WuDunn

With Pulitzer Prize winners Nicholas D. Kristof and Sheryl WuDunn as our guides, this book undertakes an odyssey through Africa and Asia to meet the extraordinary women struggling there, among them a Cambodian teenager sold into sex slavery and an Ethiopian woman who suffered devastating injuries in childbirth. Kristof and WuDunn depict our world with anger, sadness, clarity, and, ultimately, hope, and they help us see that the key to economic progress lies in unleashing women's potential. They make clear how so many people have helped to do just that, and how we can each do our part. Deeply felt, pragmatic, and inspirational, *Half the Sky* is essential reading for every global citizen.

10. *The Heart of Learning: Spirituality in Education* (1999) – by Steven Glazer

This extraordinary collection of original work provides a unified, inspiring, and immensely practical new paradigm for how teaching and learning can mean more, accomplish more, and inspire the best in each of us. This book is a must for every teacher, student, parent, and anyone who loves to learn.

11. *How to Be Compassionate: A Handbook for Creating Inner Peace and a Happier World* (2011) – by the 14th Dalai Lama and Jeffrey Hopkins

In *How to Be Compassionate*, His Holiness reveals basic mistakes of attitude that lead us to inner turmoil, and how we can correct them to achieve a better tomorrow. Enlivened by personal anecdotes and intimate accounts of the Dalai Lama's experiences as a student, thinker, political leader, and Nobel Peace Prize Laureate, *How to Be Compassionate* gives seekers of all faiths the keys to overcoming anger, hatred, and selfishness—the primary obstacles to happiness—and to becoming agents of positive transformation in our communities and the world at large.

12. *Living on a Dollar a Day: The Lives and Faces of the World's Poor* (2014) – by Thomas A. Nazario

Slightly over one billion people on the planet live on a dollar a day. While the reasons for their poverty may be different, the results are much the same. Extreme poverty robs people of options in life, and the cycle is nearly impossible to break without help. *Living on a Dollar a Day* shares the personal stories of some of the poorest of the poor, honoring their lives and their struggles, and encouraging action in those who can help. In making this beautiful and moving book, a team traveled to four continents, conducted numerous interviews, and researched information on the agencies around the world that strive to help the destitute. This important book is a powerful call to action for anyone who wishes to help alleviate human suffering.

13. *Material World: A Global Family Portrait* (1995) – by Peter Menzel

In an unprecedented effort, 16 of the world's foremost photographers traveled to 30 nations around the globe to live for a week with families that were statistically average for that nation. Vividly portraying the look and feel of the human condition everywhere on earth, this internationally acclaimed bestseller puts a human face on the issues of population, environment, social justice, and consumption as it illuminates the crucial question facing our species today: Can all 6 billion of us have all the things we want?

14. *The Most Good You Can Do: How Effective Altruism Is Changing Ideas about Living Ethically* (2015) – by Peter Singer

The Most Good You Can Do develops the challenges Peter Singer has made, in the *New York Times* and *Washington Post*, to those who donate to the arts and to charities focused on helping our fellow citizens, rather than those for whom we can do the most good. Effective altruists are extending our knowledge of the possibilities of living less selfishly, and of allowing reason, rather than emotion, to determine how we live. *The Most Good You Can Do* offers new hope for our ability to tackle the world's most pressing problems.

15. *The No-Nonsense Guide to World Poverty* (2007) – by Jeremy Seabrook

Drawing on testimonies from around the world, as well as on the hard facts, Seabrook challenges the assumption that wealth overcomes poverty, and demonstrates that the opposite of "poor" is not "rich" but "self-reliant." In *The No-Nonsense Guide to World Poverty*, Seabrook gives voice to those whose views are rarely sought and shows how we all need to live more modestly to make poverty history.

16. *The Rich and the Rest of Us: A Poverty Manifesto* (2012) – by Tavis Smiley and Cornel West

As the middle class disappears and the safety net is shredded, Smiley and West, building on the legacy of Martin Luther King Jr., ask us to confront our fear and complacency with 12 poverty-changing ideas. They challenge us to re-examine our assumptions about poverty in America—what it really is and how to eliminate it now.

17. *The Road to Character* (2015) – by David Brooks

In *The Road to Character,* David Brooks focuses on the deeper values that should inform our lives. Responding to what he calls the culture of the Big Me, which emphasizes external success, Brooks challenges us, and himself, to rebalance the scales between our "résumé virtues"—achieving wealth, fame, and status—and our "eulogy virtues"—those that exist at the core of our being: kindness, bravery, honesty, or faithfulness, focusing on what kind of relationships we have formed. Looking to some of the world's greatest thinkers and inspiring leaders, Brooks explores how, through internal struggle and a sense of their own limitations, they have built a strong inner character. Blending psychology, politics, spirituality, and confessional, *The Road to Character* provides an opportunity for us to rethink our priorities, and strive to build rich inner lives marked by humility and moral depth.

18. *Stuffed and Starved: The Hidden Battle for the World Food System* (Revised and Updated 2012) – by Raj Patel

In *Stuffed and Starved,* Raj Patel discusses the intricate link between extreme wealth and extreme poverty. He asks us to think about the way our food comes to us, to understand how what we buy directly affects the world's poorest citizens, and to recognize how we ourselves are poisoned by our choices. *Stuffed and Starved* is a shocking and timely story of commercial greed, desperate hunger, and inspirational alternatives to the current food system.

19. *Tattoos on the Heart: The Power of Boundless Compassion* (2011) – by **Gregory Boyle**

For 20 years, Father Gregory Boyle has run Homeboy Industries, a gang-intervention program located in the Boyle Heights neighborhood of Los Angeles, the gang capital of the world. In *Tattoos on the Heart*, he distills his experience working in the ghetto into a breathtaking series of parables inspired by faith. These essays about universal kinship and redemption are moving examples of the power of unconditional love and the importance of fighting despair.

20. *What Matters: The World's Preeminent Photojournalists and Thinkers Depict Essential Issues of Our Time* (2008) – by **David Cohen**

What Matters asks, "What are the essential issues of our time?" The answer appears in 18 powerful, page-turning stories by the foremost photojournalists of our age and features trenchant commentary from well-recognized experts. The combination of compelling photographs and insightful writing make this a highly relevant, widely discussed book bound to appeal to anyone concerned about the crucial issues shaping our world. It will also inspire readers to do their part—however small—to make a difference.

21. *What Money Can't Buy: The Moral Limits of Markets* (2013) – by **Michael J. Sandel**

In *What Money Can't Buy*, Michael J. Sandel takes up one of the biggest ethical questions of our time: What are the moral limits of markets? Isn't there something wrong with a world in which everything is for sale? Sandel discusses the proper role of markets in a democratic society and searches for ways to protect the moral and civic goods that markets do not honor and money cannot buy.

22. *The Wisdom of Compassion: Stories of Remarkable Encounters and Timeless Insights* (2014) – by **His Holiness, the 14th Dalai Lama and Victor Chan**

The Wisdom of Compassion offers rare insights into the Dalai Lama's life and his efforts to translate compassion into action through deeply engaging, behind-the-scene stories about his interactions with remarkable people from all walks of life. Through his own conduct, he shows us the tangible benefits of practicing kindness, forgiveness, and compassion, demonstrating that opening our hearts and minds to others is the surest path to true happiness.

Appendix #3: Videos Recommended for Participants

The videos listed below have been selected and pre-screened for possible use by a facilitator in the process of going through this program and teaching the lessons. These videos would be particularly useful when presenting the subject areas covered within the lessons. All these videos are between 2 and 20 minutes or so in length and can be used in class to introduce a topic or give participants something to think about as they leave class and prepare for the next lesson. The videos are in the order that they appear in Lessons One through Nine to help you make the best use of them as you proceed through the program. All videos below are publicly available at no cost unless otherwise noted, and The Forgotten International does not own the rights to any of them.

Lesson One:

- **"First World Problems Anthem"** by WaterisLife.com (1 minute)
  www.youtube.com/watch?v=fxyhfiCO_XQ

- **"No Arms, No Legs, No Worries"** by Nick Vujicic, edited by HumplePie Ent. (4 minutes)
  https://www.youtube.com/watch?v=ciYk-UwqFKA

- **"Gratitude"** by Gratitude HDMoving Art™ (6 minutes)
  www.youtube.com/watch?v=nj2ofrX7jAk

Lesson Two:

- **"The Miniature Earth"** (2010 edition), official version by Al Lucca (3 minutes)
  www.youtube.com/watch?v=i4639vev1Rw

- **"Call Me Hope"** by Mamahope.org (2 minutes)
  www.youtube.com/watch?v=OzQfFcy3KJg

- **"The Sharing Experiment"** by Action Against Hunger (2 minutes)
  www.youtube.com/watch?v=zFTspq_nzG4

Lesson Three:

- **"What Is a Human Right?"** by UN Human Rights (2 minutes)
  www.youtube.com/watch?v=JpY9s1Agbsw

Lesson Four:

- **"Homeless Boy Steals the Talent Show"** by Korea's Got Talent, TVN (8 minutes)
  www.youtube.com/watch?v=tZ46Ot4_ILo

- **"Children Full of Life: Part One"** by typoprone (10 minutes)
  www.youtube.com/watch?v=armP8TfS9ls

- **"Children Full of Life – Important Documentary"** by typoprone (40 minutes)
  https://www.youtube.com/watch?v=1tLB1IU-H0M
- **"Sometimes You're a Caterpillar"** by Chescaleigh and Kat Blaque (3 minutes)
  www.youtube.com/watch?v=hRiWgx4sHGg

Lesson Five:

- **"22 Random Acts of Kindness"** by Syed Muzamil Hasan Zaidi (3 minutes)
  www.youtube.com/watch?v=wskG18saKk0

- **"2013 Kindness Challenge Winner-Hannah Brencher, More Love Letters"**
  by Random Acts of Kindness (4 minutes)
  www.youtube.com/watch?v=h6VgNzJ04z8

- **"LA Man Loans House to Homeless Family for One Year"** by Go Inspire Go (4 minutes)
  https://www.youtube.com/watch?v=dOwMGYyGK7M

- **"Act of Sportsmanship Gives Texas High Schooler Shot at Glory"**
  by Steve Hartman, CBS (3 minutes)
  www.youtube.com/watch?v=5rOhn1hkkok

Lesson Six:

- **"Living on a Dollar a Day"** by The Forgotten International (4 minutes)
  www.theforgottenintl.org/build-awareness/living-on-a-dollar-a-day-the-documentary

Lesson Seven:

- **"CNN: Feeding the Hungry, Nourishing the Soul"** by CNN (3 minutes)
  www.youtube.com/watch?v=ZiC_9RHTvsA

- **"Back on My Feet"** by Storytellers For Good (5 minutes)
  www.vimeo.com/38675251

Lesson Eight:

- **"Story of Stuff"** (2007, Official Version) by The Story of Stuff Project (22 minutes)
  www.storyofstuff.org/movies/story-of-stuff

Lesson Nine:

- **"Pursuit of Happyness - Ending Scene"** by Ciprian Vatamanu (5 minutes)
  https://www.youtube.com/watch?v=x8-7mHT9edg

Lesson Ten:

- **"Pre-School Kindness"** by Random Acts of Kindness (3 minutes)
  www.youtube.com/watch?v=JRaBKR6EKow

Appendix #4: Videos Recommended for Viewing by Group Leaders or Facilitators

1. The Center for Compassion and Altruism Research and Education

The Center for Compassion and Altruism Research and Education (CCARE) at the Stanford School of Medicine offers several videos on compassion, including lectures from conferences and a speakers series. **ccare.stanford.edu/video**

2. *Hope and Compassion* (2003)

Hope and Compassion by Michel Gardey presents personalities of compassion in action and explores how this practice has changed their lives. "Compassion eliminates fear. Let authentic and pure compassion grow in us in place of hatred and fear. If fear disappears, then confidence and inner peace will resurface," notes the 14th Dalai Lama.
www.cultureunplugged.com/play/8389/Hope-and-Compassion

3. *Mighty Times: A Children's March* (2004)

The Children's March tells the story of how the young people of Birmingham, Alabama, braved fire hoses and police dogs in 1963 and brought segregation to its knees. Their heroism complements discussions about the ability of today's young people to be catalysts for positive social change.

Teachers can order this film for free with a teacher's guide for appropriate grade levels through the Teaching Tolerance website:
www.tolerance.org/kit/mighty-times-childrens-march

4. *Pray the Devil Back to Hell* (2008)

Pray the Devil Back to Hell chronicles the remarkable story of the Liberian women who came together to end a bloody civil war and bring peace to their shattered country. Thousands of women—ordinary mothers, grandmothers, aunts, and daughters, both Christian and Muslim—came together to pray for peace and then staged a silent protest outside of the Presidential Palace. Armed only with white T-shirts and the courage of their convictions, they demanded a resolution to the country's civil war. Their actions were a critical element in bringing about an agreement during the stalled peace talks. Inspiring, uplifting, and, most of all, motivating, it is a compelling testimony of how grassroots activism can alter the history of nations.
www.forkfilms.net/pray-the-devil-back-to-hell/

5. Why Poverty?

Why Poverty? features eight documentaries from award-winning filmmakers and 34 short films from new and emerging talents shown around the world in 2012. The films are thought-provoking stories that tackle big issues and pose difficult questions. The documentaries are all free to view online and download. They're currently available in Spanish and English. There is also Facilitator's/Educator's Guide PDF available. **www.vimeo.com/whypoverty**

Appendix #5: Movies That Are Worth Watching: Feature Films

1. *The Blind Side* – 2009 (Lessons 5 and 10)

The Blind Side is based on the true story of Leigh Anne and Sean Tuohy from Memphis, Tennessee, who take in a homeless teenager named Michael "Big Mike" Oher. Michael has lived a difficult life and had little formal education or family support. Leigh Anne takes it upon herself to ensure that Michael has every opportunity to succeed. With the Tuohy family's support, Michael is able to improve his grades to the point where he qualifies for an NCAA Division I athletic scholarship. This movie reveals how compassion and generosity can change the lives of everyone involved.

Essential Questions:

- *In what ways does the Tuohy family show Michael compassion beyond simply taking him into their home?*
- *What does the Tuohy family learn about life from Michael?*
- *How does Michael change their lives as well?*
- *How does this movie demonstrate the reciprocal nature of compassion?*

2. *Coach Carter* – 2005 (Lesson 10)

Coach Carter tells the story of Ken Carter, a successful sporting goods store owner who accepts the job of basketball coach for his old high school in a poor area of Richmond, California, where he was a champion athlete. Carter sets out to improve his players' basketball skills, shift their attitudes, and build their characters all at the same time. He also emphasizes the importance of getting a good education. *Coach Carter* is a great example of how a single person's compassion and conviction can transform the lives of a group of young people others had written off.

Essential Questions:

- *What qualities of a leader does Coach Carter exhibit throughout the movie?*
- *How does Coach Carter show compassion toward his players?*
- *What does Coach Carter teach his players about life and how does he help build their moral characters?*

3. *Freedom Writers* – 2007 (Lessons 5, 6, and 7)

Freedom Writers is based on the true story of one young teacher who uses education to transform the lives and futures of inner-city youth in Long Beach, California. This film does a relatively accurate job of portraying the complicated lives of students growing up in violent urban communities. As long as the movie is presented in a respectful way where stereotypes are addressed, it can serve as a tool for exposing privileged youth to the challenges of teens living not too far away from them. In addition, *Freedom Writers* explores relevant topics such as moral responsibility and diversity. Compassion is a significant theme in the movie, as the inner-city youth develop deep empathy for victims of the Holocaust and learn to care for one another despite ethnic differences and opposing gang affiliations.

Essential Questions:

- *Contrast these students' lives from your own. What challenges do they face?*
- *How do students overcome their differences throughout the movie?*
- *What lesson does their story teach us about the power of love and unity to overcome violence and hate?*
- *What impact does learning about the Holocaust have on the students? How does this relate to the theme of empathy?*

4. *Gandhi* – 1982 (Lessons 4, 5, and 10)

This movie, based on the real life of one of history's most revered leaders, Mohandas Gandhi, tells the story of how one man used compassion as a tactical and philosophical approach to overcome oppression and, in the process, united and liberated an entire nation. This movie does a remarkable job of illustrating Gandhi's peaceful nature and explaining just what a powerful presence he was in India and around the world. This movie has been used widely at both the high school and university level in conjunction with lessons on nonviolence and the history of India.

Curriculum for the movie can be found on various websites, including Gandhi: The Curriculum Project:
www.curriculumproject.org/wp-content/uploads/Gandhi.pdf

Essential Questions:

- *Explain Gandhi's philosophy on nonviolence. How does Gandhi use nonviolence to overcome oppression in India?*
- *How does Gandhi use compassion to unite the people of India?*
- *Explain how the principle of compassion led to the liberation of India from British sovereignty.*

5. *The Impossible* – 2012 (Lessons 5 and 10)

The Impossible is based on the true story of a tourist family in Thailand caught in the destruction and chaotic aftermath of the 2004 Indian Ocean tsunami. Literally torn apart by an enormous wave, the movie shows how the various members of the family search for one another while fighting for their own survival. This movie does a wonderful job of demonstrating how horrific crises often lead to extraordinary acts of compassion. It is in our world's most devastating times that people truly extend themselves—whether that is by opening their homes to the wounded, volunteering at a makeshift hospital, aiding people in search of loved ones, or providing a shoulder to grieve on.

Essential Questions:

- *What are some examples of random acts of kindness committed in this movie?*

*- How do others help the family members, and how do the family members
   help others?*

- What does this movie reveal about the nature of people?

- How might this movie demonstrate the power of compassion?

6. *It's a Wonderful Life* – 1946 (Lessons 1 and 9)

It's a Wonderful Life is the Christmas classic about a discouraged man named George Bailey, who, on the brink of suicide, gets a glimpse of what the world would be like if he never lived. This revelation gives him renewed faith in himself and a deeper appreciation for his "ordinary" life in the fictional town of Bedford Falls. George also comes to recognize his own heroism. This movie illustrates how happiness stems not from wealth but from relationships and living a compassionate life.

Essential Questions:

- What does George learn about happiness?

- How does George's definition of heroism change over the course of the movie?

- How is he a hero himself?

- What does this movie teach us about appreciation and gratitude?

7. *Pay It Forward* – 2000 (Lessons 5 and 10)

Pay It Forward demonstrates the power of an individual to change the world through compassion. The movie begins when Trevor McKinney, a troubled seventh grader in Las Vegas, Nevada, sets out to complete a social studies assignment: Think of something to change the world and put it into action. Trevor's idea is quite simple—if he commits three significant acts of kindness for three different people and then asks in return that they "pay it forward" by doing something nice for three other people, then kindness will eventually go viral. Over the course of the movie, we witness the exponential effects of Trevor's plan and recognize that, yes, something as simple as being kind can, perhaps, change the world.

Curriculum corresponding to *Pay It Forward* can be found on the web, including at the website, "Learning to Give": **http://www.learningtogive.org/units/grow-involved-9-12/pay-it-forward-grade-9**

Essential Questions:

- Explain Trevor's "pay it forward" idea.

*- How does Trevor's plan rely on the basic goodness of people?
   Do people live up to his ideal?*

- In the end, does Trevor succeed in making a difference?

- In your opinion, can compassion change the world?

8. *The Pursuit of Happyness* – 2006 (Lessons 7 and 9)

The Pursuit of Happyness is based on the true story of Christopher Gardner, a man who, due to a string of bad luck, finds himself an unemployed single dad without a home in San Francisco, California. Over the course of the movie, we see Christopher battle against the odds to create a better life for himself and his son. His is another version of the American dream and what it means to pursue happiness. This movie also effectively demonstrates that homelessness is often about unlucky circumstances, not a lack of will and ability. It cautions against blanket judgments and encourages us to give everyone a chance.

Essential Questions:

- *What set of circumstances lead Gardner to homelessness?*
- *How do you think Gardner would define happiness?*
- *How is Gardner's background different from the stockbrokers at Dean Witter?*
- *How is he similar to them?*
- *What do you think is the moral of this movie? What does it teach you about life and the pursuit of happiness?*

9. *Slumdog Millionaire* – 2008 (Lessons 2 and 6) *This move is rated R. Please obtain parental permission before viewing.*

Slumdog Millionaire is the fictional story of a teen from the slums of Mumbai, India, who becomes a contestant on the Indian version of *Who Wants to Be a Millionaire?* He is arrested under suspicion of cheating and, while being interrogated, events from his life are shown which explain how he knows the answers. This movie is a helpful classroom tool for a number of reasons. First, it does a good job of portraying the reality of poverty in Indian slums. Second, it demonstrates how everyone, regardless of wealth, strives for goodness, success, and a better life.

Essential Questions:

- *Describe the slums of Mumbai. In what different ways does poverty affect the lives of the people who live there?*
- *What additional hardships do children who grow up in the slums face on account of their poverty?*
- *What role does morality play in* Slumdog Millionaire *and the fate of the protagonist?*
- *What lesson does this movie teach about the commonality of all people?*

10. *The Soloist* – 2009 (Lessons 6, 7, and 10)

The Soloist begins when a successful *Los Angeles Times* columnist, Steve Lopez, meets Nathaniel Ayers, a mentally ill, homeless street musician who possesses extraordinary musical talent. Inspired by his story, Lopez writes an acclaimed series of articles about Ayers and attempts to do more to help both him and the rest of the "invisible" homeless communities of Los Angeles have a better life. This movie is a great way to expose participants to the realities of homelessness and the larger social injustices facing others like Ayers. It does a good job of confronting stereotypes about both the homeless and the mentally ill, and it also demonstrates how a single person committed to a cause can create change.

Curricula centered around *The Soloist* can be found on the web, including at:
www.takepart.com/sites/default/files/The-Soloist-Educational-Resource-Guide.pdf

Essential Questions:

- *What does Lopez discover about the lives of the homeless through his relationship with Ayers?*

- *How does Ayers's portrayal of mental illness compare to other portrayals of the mentally ill you've seen in the past?*

- *What does Steve Lopez do to improve the lives of the poor in Los Angeles?*

Appendix #6: Movies That Are Worth Watching: Documentaries

1. *An Inconvenient Truth* – 2006 (Lesson 8)

In this popular environmental documentary, director Davis Guggenheim weaves the science of global warming with Al Gore's personal history and lifelong commitment to reversing the effects of global climate change. A longtime advocate for the environment, Gore presents a wide array of facts and information in a thoughtful and compelling way. *An Inconvenient Truth* is not a story of despair, but rather a rallying cry to protect the one Earth we all share. This documentary is an engaging way to get kids interested in environmental studies.

Essential Questions:

- *In a few sentences, what is Al Gore's overall message about global warming?*
- *What are some new or surprising facts about global warming you learned by watching this film?*
- *What can you personally do to protect our environment and change the course we are currently on?*

2. *A Small Act* – 2010 (Lessons 5, 6, and 10)

A Small Act is about Chris Mburu, a Harvard Law School graduate who returns to his native country of Kenya to start a scholarship program. The documentary focuses on the stories of three promising students in Mburu's program as they aspire to follow his footsteps. In the film he also searches for and expresses his gratitude toward the Swedish woman who sponsored his own education. This documentary does a great job of showing all of the different variables that make getting an education in an impoverished community so difficult. It also demonstrates how the generosity of a single person can transform lives.

Related Resources: **http://www.networkforgood.com/nonprofitblog/asmallact/** and **www.asmallact.com/takeaction.php**

Essential Questions:

- *What does this film demonstrate about the challenges of students growing up in rural Kenya?*
- *What aspects of these children's lives interfere with their dreams of going to college?*
- *How is this story an example of "paying forward" compassion?*
- *Who in the movie demonstrates compassion for others? How do their compassionate acts change lives?*

3. *Born into Brothels* – 2004 (Lessons 5, 6, and 7)

Born Into Brothels is a documentary about a photographer/photojournalist, Zana Briski, who goes to India to do a story on one of the red light districts of Calcutta. She develops a relationship with some of the kids who live there and ends up teaching them how to make pictures. She then gives them cameras to take photographs of their every day lives, the proceeds of which go to fund their educations. This documentary spreads awareness of the plight of so many women born into prostitution and at the same time provides hope for their futures.

Companion Curriculum can be found on the Amnesty International website at: **www.amnesty.org/en/documents/sec01/0004/2013/en/**

Essential Questions:

- *Explain the meaning and implications of the film's title.*
  What does it reveal about the cyclical nature of poverty?
- *Describe the children in the film. What are their interests? Dreams? Abilities?*
- *How are they both different from and similar to youth in America?*
- *How does Zana continue to make a difference in these and other children's lives?*

4. *Cowspiracy: The Sustainability Secret* – 2014 (Lesson 10)

For those groups or individuals that are motivated by issues which relate more to sustainability, the care of our environment, and/or animal welfare, this documentary may inspire them to undertake a project that will encourage others to begin to care more for Mother Earth and all the species that share this planet with us.

To request a screening or download the film: **http://www.cowspiracy.com/**

Essential Questions:

- *What did you learn that you didn't already know after watching this film?*
- *What do you think is the most important thing one could do to help save the world?*

5. *The End of Poverty?* – 2008 (Lessons 2, 3, 6, and 7)

The End of Poverty? explores global poverty through history up to the present day. It examines the devastating effects of colonization on many populations across the world and analyzes the causes of extreme wealth inequality today. This documentary is particularly useful in classes centered around globalization, international studies, or economics, as it provides a very thorough analysis of today's global economy. It also discusses potential solutions to eradicate the epidemic of poverty in our world and gives viewers direct advice as to how to create change.

You can order a companion curriculum book at: **http://www.theendofpoverty.com/companion-book.html**

Essential Questions:

- *What is the thesis presented in this film?*
- *How do the experts in this film explain the origins of poverty? In other words, who is to blame?*

- What solutions do they suggest for the eradication of poverty? What steps do they recommend we take in order to create a more just global economy?

6. *Girl Rising* – 2013 (Lessons 6, 7, and 10)

Girl Rising tells the stories of nine girls from different parts of the world who face arranged marriages, child slavery, and other heartbreaking injustices. By getting an education, they're able to break barriers and create change. *Girl Rising* showcases the strength of the human spirit and the power of education to change the world.

To request a screening or to buy or download the DVD, visit the *Girl Rising* website: **www.10x10act.org/girl-rising**

Essential Questions:

- What different obstacles do the girls in the film face?

- How does education change their lives?

- In what ways do these girls show bravery and strength?

- What is the overall message of this film? How well do you think it is conveyed?

7. *Happy* – 2013 (Lessons 1 and 9)

The documentary *Happy* explores the secret behind our most valued emotion, happiness, by combining real-life stories of people from around the world and interviews with the leading scientists in happiness research. Not only does it dispel many myths about what brings people happiness, but it also gives the viewer insights as to how to live a happier life. This documentary is both educational and engaging, and it is a great way to build participants' emotional intelligence and happiness quotient.

Related resources: **http://www.thehappymovie.com/**

Essential Questions:

- What do the experts say about the correlation between wealth and happiness? Does this surprise you?

- Who are some of the happiest people profiled in the film? What makes them happy?

- What is the relationship between happiness and compassion?

- According to the film, what are some keys to long-term happiness?

8. *Living on One Dollar* – 2013 (Lessons 6, 8, and 10)

This documentary follows four friends from the United States as they spend their summer living in Guatemala on one dollar a day to try to understand the reality of poverty firsthand. This movie could provide great insight into both the lives of the very poor and the experience of living in poverty. It is also an example of young people getting involved in the fight against poverty.

To request a screening, download the film, or to learn more about Living on One's poverty alleviation efforts, please visit: **www.LivingonOne.org/film**

- *What motivated these young men to take on this project? What were their intentions and expectations going into the project?*

- *What insights into poverty did the friends obtain from their interactions with the local people and their observations of the way the local people lived?*

- *What insights did the friends obtain from the experience of living on such a meager budget?*

- *As a result of their experience, how do the friends plan on making a difference in the lives of the very poor?*

9. *On the Way to School (Sur le chemin de l'école)* – 2013 (Lessons 1, 4, and 6)

Directed by Pascal Plisson, this film tells the story of what some children around the world do to simply get to school and acquire an education. It is truly heartwarming and enlightening, often placing the viewer in the shoes of the children depicted in this film.

Essential Questions:

- *What, if anything, surprised you in the film?*

- *Did you at any point feel for these children?*

- *Which one?*

- *Do you feel any differently about your school and the education you are receiving?*

10. *The Revolutionary Optimists* – 2013 (Lessons 3, 6, 7, and 10)

In the slums of Kolkata (Calcutta), India, the kids live in unimaginable poverty, but one educated Bengali man, attorney Amlan Ganguly, believes that they have the potential to make a change in the world. Ganguly encourages tweens and teens to rise above their circumstances and educate people about their plight—such as their lack of access to clean water. *The Revolutionary Optimists* not only exposes participants to the plights of those living in extreme poverty but also demonstrates that no matter how poor or young someone might be, they can do more than just dream of a better future.

Related Web Resource: **www.revolutionaryoptimists.org/map-your-world**

Essential Questions:

- *Describe life in the Calcutta slums. What challenges do the children growing up there face?*

- *How is Amlan Ganguly a hero?*

- *What does this movie show about the empowerment of children? How are these kids changing their community?*

11. *Stolen Childhoods* – 2005 (Lessons 3, 4, and 6)

Stolen Childhoods was one of the first feature documentaries on global child labor ever produced. The film investigates the lives of child laborers around the world and gives the children an opportunity to tell their stories in their own words. The film also places these children's stories in the broader context of the worldwide struggle against child labor. *Stolen Childhoods* is a great teaching tool, as it provides an understanding of the causes of child labor, what it costs the global community, how it contributes to global insecurity, and what it will take to eliminate it. The film also shows programs that remove children from work and put them in schools so that they have a chance to develop as children and lead better futures.

To purchase the film and for related resources, see Galen Films:
http://galenfilms.com/?page_id=64

Essential Questions:

- *Choose one or two featured children and describe their living and working conditions.*

- *Think about the title of the film. In what different ways are these kids' childhoods "stolen" from them?*

- *In what ways are people around the world working to combat global child labor?*

12. *Waste Land* – 2010 (Lessons 5, 6, and 7)

Waste Land is an uplifting documentary that highlights the transformative power of art and the beauty of the human spirit. Top-selling contemporary artist Vik Muniz takes us on an emotional journey from Jardim Gramacho, the world's largest landfill on the outskirts of Rio de Janeiro, to the heights of international art stardom. The film portrays the lives of the garbage pickers and their working conditions as well as Muniz's efforts to help them to gain recognition and better living conditions.

Essential Questions:

- *Describe the conditions of the garbage pickers in Rio de Janeiro.*

- *How is Vik Muniz a success story? How does he use his success to give back to his home country?*

- *How does Vik Muniz use art and compassion to change the lives of others?*

Appendix #7: Recommended Websites

1. Advent Conspiracy: www.adventconspiracy.org

This website has resources on ways to get involved in helping others around the world. There is also a curriculum that asks important questions about giving and receiving, especially near Christmas time. It is a faith-based organization, but much of the material can be used to present poignant questions to participants that challenge consumerism and the world we live in.

2. American Humanist (for Educators): www.khec.americanhumanist.org

This website has a curriculum for teachers on morality and humanitarianism. There are useful links and documents for teaching in classroom settings, as well as thoughts and values on humanism for educators.

3. The Center for Compassion and Altruism Research and Education: ccare.stanford.edu

CCARE at the Stanford School of Medicine investigates methods for cultivating compassion and promoting altruism within individuals and society through rigorous research, scientific collaborations, and academic conferences. In addition, CCARE provides a compassion cultivation program and teacher training as well as educational public events and programs.

4. Facing the Future: www.facingthefuture.org

This website offers an already created curriculum for educators to offer their students that ties everyday subject matter into a global theme. This curriculum engages students in learning and empowers them to take action in their schools and communities.

5. The Forgotten International: www.theforgottenintl.org

The Forgotten International is the San Francisco–based foundation which created the Compassion Education Project. From this website you can be linked to a page specifically created for this program called "Doing Good." You will find additional curriculum ideas and other aids or suggestions to help you manage your way through this program and encourage young people to do good.

6. 40 Chances: www.40chances.com

This website is attached to Howard G. Buffett's foundation and book, *40 Chances: Finding Hope in a Hungry World*, and is intended to give readers and those interested ways to take action and to get involved in making the world a better place and help ease the suffering of so many. The book itself is written in a unique format: 40 stories that will provide readers a compelling look at Buffett's travels and lessons learned, ranging from his own backyard to some of the most difficult and dangerous places on Earth.

7. Free Rice: www.freerice.com

This website is created by the United Nations World Food Program and its goal is to provide free education to all and help end world hunger. There are games on the site that are education based, and the more you play, the more rice you can raise to be given to those who are hungry. There are statistics and curriculum links for teachers as well.

8. The Girl Effect: www.girleffect.org

This website focuses on girls around the world and the challenges they face as well as how partnering with girls can impact the world because of how important young girls are in shaping the world as we know it. There are social media connections that teachers may be able to use to connect their classrooms and communicate with young people around the world.

9. Global Nomads Group: www.gng.org/program-pathways

Global Nomads Group's mission is to foster dialogue and understanding among the world's youth by bringing the world to the classroom via interactive technology. They enable conversations between middle school and high school students who otherwise would not meet. These exchanges promote empathy, peace, and build 21st-century workforce skills. Their programs are easy to incorporate into civics and social studies lessons because GNG provides pre- and post-videoconference resources that range from project-based to service-learning activities.

10. Greater Good: The Science of a Meaningful Life: www.greatergood.berkeley.edu

The Greater Good Science Center studies the psychology, sociology, and neuroscience of well-being, and teaches skills that foster a thriving, resilient, and compassionate society. Not only do they sponsor groundbreaking scientific research into social and emotional well-being, but they also help people apply this research to their personal and professional lives.

11. Kids Can Make a Difference: www.kidscanmakeadifference.org/index.php

This website has an educational program for middle and high school students that focuses on the root causes of hunger and poverty, the people most affected, solutions, and how young people can help. The major goal is to stimulate the students to make some definite follow-up action plans as they begin to realize that one person can make a difference.

12. Learning to Give: www.learningtogive.org

Learning to Give, the curriculum division of GenerationOn (www.generationon.org), is the world's leading developer of lessons and resources that teach giving and volunteerism, civic engagement, and character through service learning.

13. Make Poverty History: www.makepovertyhistory.org/schools

This website offers lots of useful ideas and resources for teaching about poverty and related global issues, including books, videos, posters, websites, and teaching kids about trade, aid, and debt. Many resources are free, and you can search by subject, age group, and country, as well as by theme.

14. Millennium Development Goals: www.un.org/millenniumgoals/reports.shtml

This website contains statistics on the 2015 Millennium Goals created by the United Nations. There are sections relating to each goal and lists of organizations that are working to eradicate extreme poverty in each area beyond 2015.

15. Poverty Program: www.povertyprogram.com/statistics.php

This website has statistics on the extent of global poverty.

16. The Random Acts of Kindness Foundation: www.randomactsofkindness.org

This is a great website for educators. It has stories about how acts of kindness have changed people's lives even when performed by ordinary individuals and not large organizations. The site has helpful resources and curriculum material for schools. There is a place to submit examples of acts of kindness that have affected your life or the life of someone you know. It would be a good daily site to look at and integrate into one's curriculum.

17. Rustic Pathways: www.rusticpathways.com

Rustic Pathways is a pioneer in providing superior quality travel and service programs for students and families in some of the world's most welcoming countries. Rustic Pathways demands professionalism and integrity across all of its operations, insists on quality in all aspects of its programs, and places the safety of its students above all other considerations. It empowers students through innovative and responsible travel experiences to positively impact lives and communities around the world.

18. Seeds of Compassion: www.seedsofcompassion.org/educators

Seeds of Compassion is a unique opportunity for teachers, principals, and superintendents to learn how education and guidance in compassion and empathy can have a real impact on children's academic performance and social and emotional skills. The Seeds event, as well as this website, provides examples of classroom curricula as well as real-world case studies that bring home to youth the importance of caring.

19. Start Empathy: www.startempathy.org

Start Empathy, an initiative of Ashoka, is a community of individuals and institutions dedicated to building a future in which every child masters empathy. The community supports student-powered learning projects and prioritizes empathy and change-making in our schools, and it provides resources to parents, educators, and students.

20. Storytellers for Good: www.storytellersforgood.com

This website not only has videos that are inspirational and motivational but also promotes ways to partake in good works and explains why it is important to help others. Moreover, it has a lot of helpful links to ways people are making a difference in the universe and how to get involved.

21. TisBest: www.tisbest.org

TisBest Charity Gift Cards empower your gift recipients to support good causes *they* are passionate about. The TisBest Charity Gift Card is a donation gift that works like a conventional gift card, but, instead of buying stuff, the recipient "spends" the TisBest card by selecting which of their 300+ charity partners receives the money. Personalize any TisBest card with your own message, image, and/or company branding.

22. United Nations: www.un.org/en/sections/resources/students/index.html

This website contains resources and curriculum provided by the UN that pertains to global issues and can be used to teach young people about the current status of the world and the biggest world issues.

23. WE Day: www.we.org/we-day/

WE Day is a celebration of youth making a difference in their local and global communities. The WE Schools Program is a year-long program that nurtures compassion in young people and gives them the tools to create transformative social change. WE Day and WE Schools is part of WE.org, which empowers people to change the world. WE.org even offers volunteer trips abroad for young people to get involved with changing the world for the better.

24. Where There Be Dragons: www.wheretherebedragons.com

Where There Be Dragons encourages the deep immersion of participants into strikingly different physical and cultural landscapes, combining the best in experiential education, travel, service learning, and physically and intellectually challenging experiences. A great way to learn about our neighbors throughout the world.

25. Zynga: www.zynga.org

This website has online games that kids can play to help raise money for nonprofit organizations that help people in developing areas of the world. This may be a good site for educators who wish to keep kids entertained, yet involved in helping to address some of the problems in the world.

Appendix #8: Fundraising Ideas

Often when you are trying to help others, or assist in some way in furthering a good cause, two things are helpful to have at your disposal: first, the time and energy that you donate to the project (your service) and, second, the money or at least the ability or wherewithal to raise some money. To that end, and in order to assist you in this endeavor, below are several ways in which young people can raise money in and around their community and school in furtherance of a good cause.

Note: When such activities are done at schools, it is important to check with teachers and/or school administrators to make sure that no local laws or school rules will be violated in the process of doing good. Remember, too, that it is important to work cooperatively with your classmates and in teams, with each team having a specific responsibility with timelines and someone leading the process at the top. Be creative and do the best job you can. You can always improve on your efforts as you continue to work to help others.

- **Auction:**

If someone were to donate a very attractive item to the school community, for example, a weekend at a resort hotel, tickets to a local show, a new laptop, or dinner at a nice restaurant, many raffle tickets could likely be sold to teachers, students, and parents, and a considerable amount of money could be raised. The raffle ticket should be drawn in public, possibly as part of another campus event—for example, at a Fundraising Dinner (see below).

- **Bake Sale:**

Students choose a given day, often when there will be a lot of people at school, maybe during a sports event or some kind of special event which has brought the entire school community to campus. Create some signs which make it clear that the sale is for a good cause, and sell as many treats as you can to maximize your profit by the day's end. The sweets are typically baked by the students who will be selling them.

- **Book Sale:**

Here, upperclassmen would sell their books to entering students. These books would, of course, be sold at a discount because they would be second hand. Nevertheless, one could raise a substantial amount of money since students need to buy these books for their classes, and the incoming students would save a substantial amount of money if they purchase their books at a discount. Proceeds from the book sale would go to your cause.

- **Car Wash:**

Students can set up a car wash either on campus or off campus and wash cars for somewhere between $5 and $10 each, all in the hopes of raising some money over the course of a day. At some schools, where there may be a large faculty parking lot, the students can wash all of the faculty cars, and teachers would get to drive home that day in a clean car. This could all be supervised by a faculty member if the school wishes. If each faculty member paid $10 and you had 50 teachers and school administrators participate, that would be $500 raised in one day.

- **Carnivals:**

A carnival is a great way to be creative in raising money. Some activities you could charge a fee for a pie-eating contest, raffle tickets (have local businesses donate prizes), teacher dunk tank, carnival games, silent auction, face painting, and a variety of concession stands selling baked goods, candy, cotton candy, lemonade, popcorn, snow cones, etc. This would be a lot of work, but it is also great fun.

- **Coupons or Coupon Books:**

Students make up coupons to sell either individually or in a book. Coupons are good for services; for example, you can sell a coupon for four hours of babysitting services, two hours of yard cleanup, five hours of computer assistance, five hours of tutoring, or ten hours of chess instructions, music lessons, or swimming lessons. Anything the students can offer would work here. Parents, teachers, and even other students could purchase these coupons. Whoever purchases the coupons would contact the person who sold them to arrange for the services to be provided. This could also be done by way of a silent auction at another campus event.

- **Crowdfunding Competition:**

Have students form groups and come up with a cause they believe in (e.g., raising money to purchase educational supplies for a school in Siem Reap, Cambodia). Each group designs a webpage on one of the online fundraising sites, such as Indiegogo.com or GoFundMe.com, where they set a common fundraising goal and start campaigning to reach that goal. The various groups can have a competition to see who reaches the goal first, or who raises the most money at the end of the campaign. Be sure to check the rules of the crowdfunding sites to make sure everyone understands the process and the financial outcomes before getting started.

- **Fundraising Dinner:**

Students could host a dinner for parents at their school and call it "Parents Night Off." These dinners are typically meals that are easy to prepare for a large group such as pasta, salad, bread, a drink, and baked goods for dessert. Each guest would pay some amount for their dinner, with all proceeds going toward a good cause. Students, of course, would have to prepare all the food, arrange for set up and clean up of the dining area, and figure out how the meal will be served. If some entertainment were provided at dinner, that would increase the chances of people coming and likely increase the amount of money raised. This is a good opportunity to add a silent auction to the event and possibly sell raffle tickets for prizes donated to the school.

- ## Holidays:

There are so many ways to take advantage of holidays. Here are a few ideas:

Valentine's Day: Have students sell roses and candy-grams around the school. Have a concession stand at a Valentine's Day dance. Have "singing valentines" where students form song and dance groups and other students pay to have a group play or sing a love song to their sweethearts (or friends!) during school. This is a lot of fun for students.

Easter: Sell Easter baskets.

Halloween: Create a haunted house and charge an entrance fee.

Thanksgiving: Throw a potluck dinner for faculty and parents (see Fundraising Dinner) or bake pies to sell for students and faculty to take home.

Hanukkah: Sell dreidels or set up a dreidel-playing tournament and charge a small participation fee.

Christmas: Sell handmade ornaments or candy canes. Put up a Christmas tree and have students buy ornaments as donations and collect gifts under the tree to later be donated to a program in need. If permitted, students could also set up a table at the mall and offer to wrap gifts for shoppers in return for a donation for their cause.

- ## Jar-a-thon:

Here, students place jars all around the school. They could be left with teachers or school administrators in a variety of departments around the school. Those who receive a jar must place their jar in a conspicuous place in their classroom or office, and over the course of a month, try to fill the jars with as much donated money as they can. The classroom or department that raises the most money over the course of that period wins the Jar-a-thon and is given a special prize. This gets the whole school involved in raising money for a good cause and turns the event into a more competitive endeavor, whereby, at the end of the month, some class or department will be acknowledged for their generosity. Students can be encouraged to donate their leftover change from lunch or snacks they purchase at school each day.

- ## Rummage Sale:

One person's trash is another person's treasure! Have students and families donate any unwanted items they have around the house—books, music, furniture, sporting equipment, etc.—and then hold a large sale at school. Make it known that the money is going to a good cause and invite the entire school and surrounding community. Baked goods could also be sold at such an event.

- ## Show or Performance:

Students could take over the school's multipurpose room or assembly room and put on a fashion show, a karaoke performance with parents and teachers, a lip-synching contest, or a talent show whereby guests would pay a small admission fee to watch and participate in the fun. This would also be a great opportunity to have a bake sale. The price of a ticket should be high enough to raise some money, but not so high that only a few would be able to come. Hopefully parents would buy most of the tickets, or agree to match any of the money raised that evening. Participants at this event could also buy raffle tickets, and at the close of the evening, one or more donated prizes would be raffled off to raise some additional funds.

- **Students versus Faculty Game:**

This would be a great lunchtime or after-school event so the entire student body can come and watch students play the faculty at basketball or volleyball or some other team sport. Again, everyone would pay a small admission fee to watch with all proceeds going to the fundraiser. At the conclusion of the game, you could also have other games for everyone to participate in, such as a free-throw contest or a beanbag toss at a specific target at center court. Any prizes given out would, of course, be donated, and this would be a good opportunity to sell treats.

- **Walk-a-Thon:**

Here students would agree to spend part of the day walking for a cause. They would walk around the school's track, and friends, family, and others would pledge anywhere from 10 cents to $1 for every lap they walk. At the end of the day, a school official would count the number of laps they had finished, verify each student's results, and students would proceed to collect their pledges accordingly. All money would be pooled by the students participating in the walk-a-thon and the funds would be used to help a designated program. This can also be accomplished through laps in a swimming pool or simply walking around the block that encompasses the school's campus.

Appendix #9: National Organizations That Do Good

The following is a list of nonprofit organizations across the country committed to improving the lives of people in need. Many of them also provide great opportunities for young people to get involved.

- **Cards for Hospitalized Kids: www.cardsforhospitalizedkids.com**

Through handmade cards that help brighten the days of children in hospitals, Cards for Hospitalized Kids spreads hope, joy, and magic. Anyone from anywhere can get involved. Individuals and groups across the United States and the world donate their time and creativity to make the cards and send them to Cards for Hospitalized Kids for distribution in hospitals and Ronald McDonald Houses across the nation. Meet up with your friends to write the cards together and share your support and care for children who cannot get out to play.
Headquarters address: 7290 W. Devon Avenue, Chicago, IL 60631
Headquarters phone: 773-458-0431
Email: info@cardsforhospitalizedkids.com

- **Feeding America: www.feedingamerica.org/find-your-local-foodbank**

Feeding America is a network of food banks that distributes more than three billion meals each year through food pantries and meal programs throughout the United States. Volunteer at a food pantry or a soup kitchen and help to serve food, stock shelves, or otherwise provide support to keep these essential services running. The Feeding America website provides a directory to help you find your local food bank and discover different ways to help nourish those in need.
Headquarters address: 35 East Wacker Drive, Suite 2000, Chicago, IL 60601
Headquarters phone: 800-771-2303
Email: online form

- **Hungry for Music: www.hungryformusic.org/**

Hungry for Music helps children and vulnerable populations transform their lives through the gift of music. Donate musical instruments to children and veterans who would not otherwise have access to them, or volunteer to transport instruments, hang flyers, and work at their events through their service projects.
Headquarters address: 2020 Pennsylvania Ave, NW, No. 384, Washington, DC 20006
Headquarters phone: 202-674-3000
Email: contact@hungryformusic.org

- **KaBOOM!: www.kaboom.org**

Only one in four children get the recommended 60 minutes of physical activity or active play every day. KaBOOM! believes all kids should get the childhood they deserve, filled with balanced and active play, so they can thrive. Help KaBOOM! build playgrounds in low-income neighborhoods by joining a fundraising team or its Play Everywhere Challenge and ensure that all children have access to the resources they need.

Headquarters address: 4301 Connecticut Avenue NW, Suite ML-1, Washington, DC 20008
Headquarters phone: 202-659-0215
Email: online form

- ## Let's Play It Forward: www.letsplayitforward.org

Let's Play It Forward was started by a group of teens in Westchester, New York, to help charitable youth organizations and individuals in need to obtain gear necessary to play the sports they love. It began when the Westchester teens realized that they had an abundance of unused sports equipment in their garages and started calling organizations to inquire whether they could make use of it. The responses were overwhelming. Help collect and donate unused or gently used sports equipment to be distributed through their organization. For children without access to a ball, bat, or cleats, this may allow them a chance to participate in the same sports you love!
Headquarters address: P.O. Box 485, Lincolndale, NY 10540
Headquarters phone: N/A
Email: letsplayitforward@aol.com

- ## Love for the Elderly: www.lovefortheelderly.org/senior-buddies.html

So many of our elderly have no one to care for them or even someone to check in to see how they are getting on. Love for the Elderly, founded by a high school student, wants to change that. You can help by providing emotional support and learning more about a different era through participation in its Pen Pals program. Some elders may not have children or grandchildren in their lives and are lonely without family support. Make a new old friend!
Headquarters address: P.O. Box 24248, Cleveland, OH 44124
Headquarters phone: 216-269-0274
Email: contact@lovefortheelderly.org

- ## Meals on Wheels: www.mealsonwheelsamerica.org

Meals on Wheels, the mobile food clinic for the elderly, makes a huge difference in the lives of many seniors. Volunteer and help provide food and a sense of community to elderly people who may no longer be able to provide for themselves.
Headquarters address: 1550 Crystal Drive, Suite 1004, Arlington, VA 22202
Headquarters phone: 888-998-6325
Email: info@mealsonwheelsamerica.org

- ## Musicians on Call: www.musiciansoncall.org/site/PageNavigator/home

It's no secret that music is healing and can help lift the spirit, which is why Musicians on Call brings live and recorded music to the bedsides of patients in healthcare facilities. Volunteer with Musicians on Call to play a show for hospital patients or help to organize such a show. Share your musical skills and help to bring a smile to those being treated for major illnesses or injuries. You could also gather your band, dance group, or choir and contact your local hospital or senior center for permission to visit.

Headquarters address: 39 West 32nd Street, Suite 1103, New York, NY 10001
Headquarters phone: 212-741-2709
Email: info@musiciansoncall.org

- **One Warm Coat: www.onewarmcoat.org**

Even a two-degree drop in body temperature can result in reduced heart rate, loss of coordination, and confusion, making it difficult for adults to work effectively and children to learn. For many, a warm coat solves the problem. But for families of those living in poverty, a winter coat is a budget "extra." Help One Warm Coat provide coats to those in need by holding a coat drive. Cold winters can be hard enough, but for people who don't have the money for a proper coat, or even a place to stay, they are nearly impossible.
Headquarters address: 2443 Fillmore Street, San Francisco, CA 94115
Headquarters phone: 877-663-9276
Email: drives@onewarmcoat.org

- **Read Across America: www.nea.org/grants/plan-a-reading-event.htm**

Children who spend more time reading do better and are happier in school. Recognizing the important role reading plays, every year on March 2, the birthday of beloved children's author Dr. Seuss, teachers, teenagers, librarians, politicians, actors, athletes, parents, and grandparents across the nation join the National Education Association–sponsored Read Across America activities to bring reading excitement to children of all ages. Read Across America also provides ways to keep reading on the calendar all year long.
Headquarters address: 1319 F Street NW, Suite 1000, Washington, DC 20004
Headquarters phone: 202-833-4000
Email: online form

- **Special Olympics: www.specialolympics.org/Sections/Get_Involved/ Volunteer_for_Special_Olympics.aspx**

Special Olympics transforms the lives of people with intellectual disabilities through the joy of sport. Support Special Olympics' mission to show the world the capacity of those with disabilities, as well as provide them with a chance to shine. Volunteer as a coach for a variety of sports or volunteer to assist with a Special Olympics event in your area.
Headquarters address: 1133 19th Street NW, Washington, DC 20036
Headquarters phone: 202-628-3630
Email: lidaszak@specialolympics.org

- **Toys for Tots: www.toysfortots.org**

Every year, during the months of October, November, and December, Toys for Tots collects new, unwrapped toys to distribute to children who otherwise may not receive any in the communities where the campaigns are conducted. You can contribute to your local Toys for Tots campaign in several ways by donating a toy at one of your area's toy drop locations, hosting a Toys for Tots event, or volunteering at a local warehouse. Many families struggle to make ends meet and do not have the extra money to spend on toys for their children. Give them a chance to play, the same chance you had.

Headquarters address: Cooper Center, 18251 Quantico Gateway Drive, Triangle, VA 22172
Headquarters phone: 703-649-2054
Email: online form

- **YMCA: www.ymca.net/volunteer**

The YMCA's Youth Development Programs are part of the YMCA's mission to nurture the potential of every child and teen by supporting his or her unique development journey and providing the tools and resources they need to succeed in life. Volunteer with your local YMCA to help coach young children's sports teams, or tutor a child in reading or math, and build your leadership skills while helping to serve and mentor others.

Headquarters address: 101 N Wacker Drive, Chicago, IL 60606
Headquarters phone: 800-872-9622
Email: fulfillment@ymca.net

Start a Chapter Club or Connect with a Larger Organization:

- **Amnesty International: http://www.amnestyusa.org/get-involved**

Amnesty International is a global movement of people fighting injustice and promoting human rights. Start a school club and join the Amnesty International network to promote this work. You can help to improve policies around human rights issues by exposing and preventing human rights abuses through Amnesty's petitions and letter-writing campaigns.

Headquarters address: 5 Penn Plaza, 16th Floor, New York, NY 10001
Headquarters phone: 212-807-8400
Email: aimember@aiusa.org

- **Habitat for Humanity: www.habitat.org/youthprograms**

Habitat for Humanity is the largest organization working to create housing for those in need. The organization has several youth programs and accepts both short-term and long-term volunteers who go on to gain an understanding of the complexity of housing as well as supporting those in need. Their Campus Chapters are student-led organizations on high school or college campuses that partner with local Habitat affiliates.

Headquarters address: 121 Habitat Street, Americus, GA 31709
Headquarters phone: 800-HABITAT or 229-924-6935
Email: ussupportcenter@habitat.org

- **Kiva U: www.kiva.org/kivau/intro**

Kiva U envisions a world where all students and educators are empowered with tools and opportunities to become informed, inspired, and mobilized global citizens. Through experiential learning, digital collaboration, and the power of human connections, Kiva U provides a platform for young people to take action and change lives via microfinance and financial inclusion.

Headquarters address: 875 Howard Street, Suite 340, San Francisco, CA 94103
Headquarters phone: 828-479-5482
Email: online form

- **Polaris Project: www.polarisproject.org/action**

There are thousands of human trafficking victims across the United States, many of whom are children. Polaris works to restore the freedom to those trafficked and uses data and technology to uncover trafficking operations. Help them in their fight to end modern slavery by promoting political change, helping to fundraise for rescue centers, and educating others about the dangers and signs of trafficking.
Headquarters address: P.O. Box 65323, Washington, DC 20035
Headquarters phone: 202-745-1001
Email: info@polarisproject.org

- **Red Cross: www.redcross.org/volunteer/volunteer-opportunities**

The American Red Cross was founded to prevent and alleviate human suffering in the face of emergencies. Volunteers carry out 90% of the humanitarian work the organization does. Your time and talent can make a real difference in people's lives. You can volunteer with the Red Cross or create a Red Cross club at your school. For those over age 16, look into whether you are eligible to donate blood or volunteer to assist at a blood drive. A small amount of your time can help save a life.
Headquarters address: 2025 E Street NW, Washington, DC 20006
Headquarters phone: 800-RED CROSS or 800-733-2767
Email: online form

- **UNICEF: www.unicefusa.org/sites/default/files/CI15_Toolkit%20%282%29.pdf**

UNICEF works for a world in which every child has a fair chance in life. One of UNICEF's goals is to empower American youth with the resources and skills to be effective global citizens who think globally and act locally for the world's most vulnerable children. You can join the ranks of college and high school students around the country who are educating, advocating, and fundraising on behalf of UNICEF by starting a UNICEF club.
Headquarters address: 125 Maiden Lane, New York, NY 10038
Headquarters phone: 800-367-5437
Email: online form

- **WE Schools: http://we.org/we-at-school/**

WE Schools is a program that challenges young people to identify the local and global issues that spark their passion and then empowers them with the tools to take action. By becoming a WE School, or starting your own separate youth group, or even signing up with WE on your own, you can commit to working to support local and global causes. The WE program will provide you with the resources you need upon registration. You can look here to see some of the campaigns other WE School groups are involved in: **http://we.org/we-at-school/we-schools/campaigns/**.

Headquarters address: 4301 Highway 7, Suite 120, Minneapolis, MN 55416
Headquarters phone: 612-246-3311
Email: youth@we.org

Explore More Ideas:

There are many different resources for volunteer opportunities and sources for ideas to develop your own volunteer project. Below is a list of databases you can search to create your own ideas to help you get started!

Do Something: www.dosomething.org/us

Generation On: www.generationon.org/about/programs-resources

Random Acts of Kindness: www.randomactsofkindness.org/kindness-ideas

Start a Snowball: www.startasnowball.com/kids-service-project-ideas-2

VolunTEEN Nation: www.volunteennation.org/about

Youth Service America: www.ysa.org

Youth Volunteer Corps: www.yvc.org/about-us

Appendix #10: International Organizations That Do Good Around the World

When contacting one or more of these organizations, be sure to ask how you might get involved locally and whether there exists a particular school, orphanage, village, or medical clinic somewhere in the world that might benefit from your help. Below are the U.S. offices of these organizations.

- **Africare: www.africare.org**

Develops self-help programs in Africa to increase food production, develops clean water resources, manages the environment, strengthens health care, and delivers emergency assistance.
Address: Africa House, 440 R Street, NW, Washington, DC 20001
Phone: 202-464-0867
Email: info@africare.org

- **American Himalayan Foundation: www.himalayan-foundation.org**

The American Himalayan Foundation supports vital education, health care, cultural, and environmental preservation throughout the Himalayan region benefiting Tibetans and Nepalis.
Address: 909 Montgomery Street, Suite 400, San Francisco, CA 94133
Phone: 415-288-7245
Email: info@himalayan-foundation.org

- **American Jewish World Service: www.ajws.org**

Inspired by Judaism's commitment to social justice, AJWS works to realize human rights and end poverty in the developing world.
Address: 45 West 36th Street, New York, NY 10018
Phone: 212-792-2900
Email: ajws@ajws.org

- **American Near East Refugee Aid (ANERA): www.anera.org**

American Near East Refugee Aid (ANERA) is nonpolitical and nonreligious and is one of the largest American nonprofits working solely in the Middle East for 40 years.
Address: 1111 14th Street, NW, Suite 400, Washington, DC 20005
Phone: 202-266-9700
Email: anera@anera.org

- **AmeriCares: www.americares.org**

AmeriCares is an emergency response and global health organization committed to saving lives and building healthier futures for people in crisis in the United States and around the world. They restore health and save lives by delivering donated medicines, medical supplies, and humanitarian aid to people in need.

Address: 88 Hamilton Ave, Stamford, CT 06902

Phone: 203-658-9500

Email: info@americares.org

- **CARE: www.care.org**

CARE fights root causes of poverty in 84 countries with a special focus on empowering poor women to lift themselves, their families, and communities out of poverty.

Address: 465 California Street, Suite 475, San Francisco, CA 94104

Phone: 415-781-1585

Email: info@care.org

- **ChildFund International: www.childfund.org**

ChildFund International helps deprived, excluded, and vulnerable children having the capacity to become young adults and leaders who bring lasting and positive change in their communities.

Address: 2821 Emerywood Pkwy, Richmond, VA 23294

Phone: 800-776-6767

Email: questions@childfund.org

- **Children International: www.children.org**

Children International's mission is to bring lasting change to impoverished children by reducing their daily struggles and providing opportunities for better health, education, and success.

Address: 2000 East Red Bridge Road, P.O. Box 219055, Kansas City, MO 64121

Phone: 800-888-3089

Email: children@children.org

- **Church World Service: www.cwsglobal.org**

Church World Service works with partners to eradicate hunger and poverty and promote peace and justice among the world's most vulnerable people.

Address: 475 Riverside Drive, Suite 700, New York, NY 10115

Phone: 212-870-2061

Email: info@cwsglobal.org

- **Cross-Cultural Solutions: www.crossculturalsolutions.org**

Cross-Cultural Solutions is a nonprofit working to address critical global issues by providing meaningful and sustainable volunteer services to international communities and contributing responsibly to local economies. Their community-focused philosophy ensures that, as a responsible nonprofit, they are able to add real and sustainable value to the places in which

they serve, as well as provide safe and meaningful experiences to individuals seeking a volunteer abroad experience.
Address: 2 Clinton Place, New Rochelle, NY 10801
Phone: 800-380-4777
Email: info@crossculturalsolutions.org

- **Episcopal Relief & Development: www.episcopalrelief.org**

Episcopal Relief & Development is a faith-based group that works with its partners to provide relief and a compassionate response in times of disaster and promotes sustainable development by identifying and addressing the root causes of suffering.
Address: 815 Second Ave, New York, NY 10017
Phone: 855-312-4325
Email: info@episcopalrelief.org

- **Freedom From Hunger: www.freedomfromhunger.org**

Freedom from Hunger brings innovative and sustainable self-help solutions to the fight against chronic hunger and poverty. Together with local partners, they equip families with resources they need to build futures of health, hope, and dignity.
Address: 1460 Drew Ave, Suite 300, Davis, CA 95618
Phone: 530-758-6200
Email: info@freedomfromhunger.org

- **Health Volunteers Overseas: www.hvousa.org**

HVO trains, mentors, and provides critical professional support to more than 3,000 healthcare providers who care for the neediest populations in over 25 countries.
Address: 1900 L Street, NW #310, Washington, DC 20036
Phone: 202-296-0928
Email: info@hvousa.org

- **Heifer International: www.heifer.org**

Heifer helps poor families worldwide become self-sufficient by providing food, income-producing animals, and training in animal management, environmentally sound farming practices, and community development.
Address: 1 World Ave, Little Rock, AR 72202
Phone: 855-948-6437
Email: info@heifer.org

- **International Orthodox Christian Charities: www.iocc.org**

The IOCC is a faith-based organization that provides humanitarian and development assistance without discriminaton to people in the United States, Africa, Asia, Europe, and the Middle East, who have been devastated by man-made and natural disasters.
Address: 110 West Road, Suite 360, Baltimore, MD 21204

Phone: 410-243-9820
Email: relief@iocc.org

- ## Mercy Corps: www.mercycorps.org

Mercy Corps provides lifesaving aid worldwide following a disaster or conflict and helps local populations design and implement sustainable programs to promote health and economic development.
Address: 45 SW Ankeny Street, Portland, OR 97204
Phone: 503-896-5000
Email: online form

- ## Oxfam America: www.oxfamamerica.org

Oxfam America is a global organization working to right the wrongs of poverty, hunger, and injustice. They work with people in more than 90 countries to create lasting solutions to these problems. Oxfam saves lives, develops long-term solutions to poverty, and campaigns for social change.
Address: 226 Causeway Street, 5th Floor, Boston, MA 02114
Phone: 800-776-9326
Email: info@oxfamamerica.org

- ## Plan International USA: www.planusa.org

Plan International USA is part of a global organization that works with communities in 50 developing countries to end the cycle of poverty for children.
Address: 1255 23rd Street, NW, Suite 300, Washington, DC 20037
Phone: 202-617-2300
Email: online form

- ## Project HOPE: www.projecthope.org

HOPE (Health Opportunities for People Everywhere) is dedicated to providing lasting solutions to health problems with its mission to achieve sustainable advances in health care around the world by implementing health education programs and providing humanitarian assistance.
Address: 255 Carter Hall Lane, P.O. Box 250, Millwood, VA 22646
Phone: 540-837-2100
Email: online form

- ## Rotary Foundation of Rotary International: www.rotary.org

Rotary's mission is to advance world understanding, goodwill, and peace through the improvement of health, the support of education, and the alleviation of poverty.
Address: One Rotary Center, 1560 Sherman Ave, Evanston, IL 60201
Phone: 866-976-8279
Email: online form

- **Save the Children: www.savethechildren.org**

Save the Children gives children in the United States and around the world what every child deserves—a healthy start, the opportunity to learn, and care when disaster strikes. Their mission is to inspire breakthroughs in the way the world treats children and to achieve immediate and lasting change in their lives.
Address: 501 Kings Highway East, Suite 400, Fairfield, CT 06825
Phone: 203-221-4000
Email: supportercare@savechildren.org

- **SOS Children's Villages – USA: www.sos-usa.org**

The world's largest organization for orphaned and abandoned children, the SOS mission continues to build families for children in need, while helping them to shape their own futures and sharing in the development of their communities. The group's vision for the world's children is that every child should belong to a family and grow with love, respect, and security.
Address: 1620 I (Eye) Street NW, Suite 900, Washington, DC 20006
Phone: 888-767-4543
Email: online form

- **Water for People: www.waterforpeople.org**

Water for People is an international organization that supports the development of sustainable drinking water resources, sanitation facilities, and hygiene education programs in developing countries.
Address: 100 E. Tennessee Ave, Denver, CO 80209
Phone: 720-488-4590
Email: info@waterforpeople.org

- **Women for Women International: www.womenforwomen.org**

Women for Women provides direct aid, rights awareness, leadership education, vocational skills training, and income generation support to women survivors of war, conflict, and civil strife. They work with women in eight countries, offering support, tools, and access to life-changing skills to move from crisis and poverty to stability and economic self-sufficiency.
Address: 2000 M Street, NW, Suite 200, Washington, DC 20036
Phone: 202-737-7705
Email: general@womenforwomen.org

- **World Renew: www.worldrenew.net**

A faith-based group serving worldwide as the development, disaster response, and justice arm of the Christian Reformed Church in North America, the aspects of World Renew's work are threefold: community development, disaster response and rehabilitation, and advocacy for those in need.
Address: 1700 28th Street, SE, Grand Rapids, MI 49508
Phone: 616-224-0740
Email: info@worldrenew.net

Appendix #11: Books to Check Out When Deciding on a Service Project

1. ***The Complete Guide to Service Learning: Proven, Practical Ways to Engage Students in Civic Responsibility, Academic Curriculum, and Social Action (Updated)***
   Author: Cathryn Berger Kaye, MA
   Publisher: Free Spirit Publishing, 2010

This project-based guide is a blueprint for service learning—from getting started to assessing the experience—and integrates the K–12 Service-Learning Standards for Quality Practice. It provides ideas for incorporating literacy into service learning and suggestions for creating a culture of service. An award-winning treasury of activities, ideas, annotated book recommendations, author interviews, and expert essays—all presented within a curricular context and organized by theme. Digital Content contains all of the planning and tracking forms from the book, plus bonus service learning plans, and more.

2. ***Doing Good Together: 101 Easy, Meaningful Service Projects for Families, Schools, and Communities***
   Authors: Jenny Friedman, PhD, and Jolene L. Roehlkepartain
   Publisher: Free Spirit Publishing, 2010

The 101 projects in *Doing Good Together* answer the growing demand for service project ideas with hands-on projects focused on easing poverty, promoting literacy, supporting the troops, helping the environment, and more. Each of the 101 self-contained family service projects provides an overview, time requirements, materials list, step-by-step instructions, debriefing questions, recommended books to help kids and teens do or learn more, and ideas for extending the activity.

3. ***The Everyday Activist: 365 Ways to Change the World***
   Author: Michael Norton
   Publisher: House of Anansi Press, 2006

The Everyday Activist shows how even small actions can affect the local community and the wider world. Packed with ideas and facts from leading campaign organizations, this ingenious handbook suggests actions for every day of the year.

4. ***How to Make the World a Better Place: 116 Ways You Can Make a Difference***
   Authors: Linda Catling and Jeffrey Hollender
   Publisher: W.W. Norton, 2013 (Updated)

How to Make the World a Better Place, in this updated and expanded edition, shows how just one person can make a difference in solving global, national, and local problems. Whether you're interested in feeding the hungry, protecting the environment, helping the homeless, or making your community a safer place to live, you'll find the means to get started in this book. Each chapter alerts you to problems that require attention, explains the issues and what has to be done about them, tells you specifically what you can do to help, and lists the addresses and phone numbers of organizations that you can contact.

5. *It's Our World, Too! Young People Who Are Making a Difference: How They Do It—How You Can, Too!*
Author: Phillip Hoose
Publisher: Square Fish, 2002

Both a history and a handbook, this highly inspirational and engaging book will help jump-start readers who yearn to take a stand against injustice or otherwise long to make a difference. It includes a dozen-odd case studies profiling children and teens of both sexes from a variety of ethnic backgrounds who had the courage to act on their convictions. The final section of the book is a hands-on approach to mounting a personal campaign, with specific advice on such measures as starting a boycott, lobbying government officials, and raising funds—and how to do it all with creativity and flair.

6. *The Kid's Guide to Service Projects: Over 500 Service Ideas for Young People Who Want to Make a Difference*
Author: Barbara A. Lewis
Publisher: Free Spirit Publishing, 2009 (Updated)

This new edition of Free Spirit's best-selling youth service guide includes a refreshed "Ten Steps to Successful Service Projects" plus hundreds of ideas for projects—from simple to large-scale. At a time when U.S. President Barack Obama has called for increased participation in community service, this revitalized book is sure to find a whole new audience of eager young change makers.

7. *The Kid's Guide to Social Action: How to Solve the Social Problems You Choose—and Turn Creative Thinking into Positive Action*
Author: Barbara A. Lewis
Publisher: Free Spirit Publishing, 2012 (Updated)

Compelling, empowering, and packed with information, *The Kid's Guide to Social Action* is the ultimate guide for kids who want to make a difference in the world. It provides step-by-step instructions that show how to write letters, do interviews, make speeches, take surveys, raise funds, get media coverage, and more. Real stories about real kids who are doing great things let readers know they're not too young to solve problems in their neighborhood, community, and nation.

8. *Real Kids, Real Stories, Real Change: Courageous Actions Around the World*
Author: Garth Sundem
Publisher: Free Spirit Publishing, 2010

Eleven-year-old Tilly saved lives in Thailand by warning people that a tsunami was coming. Fifteen-year-old Malika fought against segregation in her Alabama town. This book is the collection of 30 true stories that profile kids who used their heads, their hearts, their courage, and sometimes their stubbornness to help others and do extraordinary things. As young readers meet these boys and girls from around the world, they may wonder, "What kind of hero lives inside of me?"

9. ***The Teen Guide to Global Action: How to Connect with Others (Near and Far) to Create Social Change***
   Author: Barbara Lewis
   Publisher: Free Spirit Publishing, 2007

The Teen Guide to Global Action includes real-life stories to inspire young readers, plus a rich and varied menu of opportunities for service, fast facts, hands-on activities, user-friendly tools, and resources kids can use to put their own volunteer spirit into practice. It also spotlights young people from the past whose efforts led to significant positive change. Upbeat, practical, and highly motivating, this book has the power to rouse young readers everywhere.

About the Authors

Thomas A. Nazario: Tom is the founder and president of The Forgotten International as well as a California attorney, child advocate, and law professor. His expertise in children's legal issues has led him to travel the world documenting human rights violations involving women and children, as well as work with inner-city kids in the Bay Area since 1978. Through these travels, he discovered many of the grassroots organizations that seek to help the poorest of the poor all over the world, and he works tirelessly to provide ongoing support to them, as well as to new organizations his foundation continues to discover. Tom leads his foundation's Board of Directors and makes presentations to community groups, colleges, foundations, and corporations that wish to get involved with the work of The Forgotten International. He is also the author of several books, including *In Defense of Children* and his most recent book, *Living on a Dollar a Day.*

Kelly Quayle: Kelly has dedicated most of her career to teaching socioeconomically disadvantaged youth in public, charter, and rural schools both locally and internationally. She recently finished the manuscript of her first book, *"Those Kids": A Year of Heartbreak and Hope on the Front Lines of Urban Education*, which chronicles her first year teaching some of the most at-risk students in Oakland, California. She also recently returned from Tetebatu, a small village in Indonesia where she spent several months teaching English, training teachers, and engaging in a variety of other projects within the community. Kelly has a BA in English from Princeton University and an MA in education from Stanford University. A strong believer in the capacity of compassion to change the world, she is excited about the potential of this project.

About The Forgotten International

The Forgotten International is a nonprofit organization founded in San Francisco, California, in 2007. It is dedicated to alleviating poverty around the world, particularly as it affects women and children. We make small grants to underserved schools and grassroots organizations, we send skilled volunteers abroad, and we try to increase awareness about global issues through projects such as this curriculum.

Although we do as much as we can, we certainly cannot remedy the many challenges that face the world's extreme poor without the help of others. Through *Doing Good*, we seek to enlist the energy and optimism of youth and challenge them to to learn more about global issues and, in doing so, decide to get involved and make the practice of doing good part of their everyday lives. It is by working together that each of us is able to accomplish far more than we can possibly do on our own. Please join this global effort, and know that our work is based on the following Twelve Simple Beliefs.

The Forgotten International's Twelve Simple Beliefs

- That all people, regardless of where they happen to be born or live, are of equal human worth and deserving of the kindness of others.

- That in women and children, who are often the most defenseless among us, lies the hope and future of the world and, for that reason, they are most in need of the world's help.

- That in giving, the giver receives as much, if not more, than he or she gives.

- That we are far more the same than different, and we should never let the differences that exist between us divide us.

- That goodness is the rule and evil the exception and, as such, we should trust in the basic goodness of all humankind.

- That ego, greed, and/or the lust for power is often responsible for much of the world's poverty and suffering. Hence these impulses should, at all cost, be resisted.

- That money is not the root of all evil but a means to an end, and that "end" can be to do good and relieve suffering. It is for us to choose.

- That the acquisition of wealth often has at least as much to do with luck and/or the service of others as a particular individual's skills, gifts, or ingenuity, and as such, one's wealth should always be shared with those less fortunate.

- That nothing cares for the world's people as much as the earth herself, and it is for that reason that the earth must be cared for in the same way that she cares for all of us. We are dependent on each other. It is a reciprocal relationship.

- That all of us have the opportunity to leave this earth better for having been here. It is what defines a meaningful life.

- That positive change often occurs through the work of many people making small contributions. Hence, there is no problem too big as long as enough people care.

- That, on occasion, all of us who live comfortable lives should step out of what we know to experience the world outside of our privileged communities. No one should be allowed to simply ignore or forget the so many all over the world that have so little and suffer so much.